MORE BOOKS BY LORI HENRY

Churchill: Navigating bugs, belugas and polar bears
Jordan: A Different Middle East
Behind My Smile: How I Recovered from an Eating Disorder
Silent Screams

Dancing Through History

Dancing Through History
In Search of the Stories that Define Canada

Lori Henry

Dancing Traveller
Publishing

Vancouver, Canada

2012 Dancing Traveller Publishing paperback edition
Dancing Traveller Publishing, Vancouver
www.DancingTravellerMedia.ca

LIBRARY AND ARCHIVES CANADA CATALOGUING IN PUBLICATION
Henry, Lori, 1982-
    Dancing through history : in search of the stories that define
Canada / Lori Henry.
Includes bibliographical references and index.
Also issued in electronic format.
ISBN: 978-0-9876897-6-4 (paperback)
ISBN: 978-0-9876897-7-1 (e-book)
    1. Henry, Lori, 1982- --Travel--Canada. 2. Dance--Canada--History.
3. Canada--Description and travel. I. Title.
GV1625.H45 2012   792.8'0971   C2012-900215-1

Printed in the United States of America

www.LoriHenry.ca

Dedication

To those whose stories have yet to be heard.

"Everybody who sings and dances knows that if they don't, no one else will."
- Margaret Grenier referring to her Gitxsan First Nations heritage

"If I don't do it, there is a chance that nobody's going to do it."
- Yvonne Chartrand on the traditional style of Métis jigging

"You are dancers, all of you. Life moves you; life *dances* you. To dance is to investigate and celebrate the experience of being alive. Like life, a dance creates and destroys itself in every moment. Like love, it is beyond reason. Ephemeral as breath, concrete as bone, dance is made of you. You sculpt space. You write with your body in a wordless language that is deeply understood. You grace the space within and around you when you dance. Force, trajectory, inertia, and recovery: dancing is a ride, a duet between your instinct and imagination. To dance is to heighten your experience of the present moment. Your body is your *location* – when you dance, you are profoundly engaged in being there."

- Crystal Pite, Canadian choreographer and performer, Kidd Pivot Frankfurt RM (excerpt from the International Dance Day message at the invitation of the Canadian Dance Assembly, March 2010)

Table of Contents

Preface

I took my first dance class when I was two years old. Some kids are given new shoes when they take their first steps, others are videotaped on their parents' camcorders for posterity. Me, I was given Polynesian dance lessons, where I learned how to swing my little hips to the beat of the Tahitian drums.

I was born with the terrifyingly harmless condition called *metatarsus adductus*, which means I was born with my feet turned in. My dad used to joke that I had had a skiing accident whenever he and my mom took me out in public with casts on both legs. The casts were a temporary step to straighten the metatarsal bone. I then had to wear specially made shoes with a bar to connect them, called DB Splints, allowing me to take only the most miniscule of steps and helping my legs learn how to develop in parallel alignment.

My doctor told my parents that there was nothing else he could do to correct my feet without surgery. His recommended training for my legs to turn out naturally was dance lessons. In his mind, ballet would organically help my lower body find its way from pigeon-toed into parallel. But at the time, no instructor would take a two-year-old-potential-brat, no matter how sweetly I smiled up at her. That is, until I met Kalaya.

Kalaya is one of those people whose character shines so stubbornly bright, your only option is to shine right along with it. She runs a Polynesian dance studio in Port Coquitlam and, when my mom asked if she would take me as a student, she made an exception to her minimum age limit because of my foot situation and said, "If she can pay attention for an hour every week, she can join us." Two lessons later and I was making my stage debut as a Polynesian dancer. Less than two years later, I was leading my dance group out on stage at Expo '86.

I credit my love of moving, my response to rhythm and my passion for performing to this early introduction to dance. It's easy to think of dance lessons as simply a means to having little girls prance around in leotards and dress up in sequenced costumes, but dance was a significant form of education for me that shaped who I was and who I have become.

Kalaya, my many ensuing teachers and, eventually, my role model, Cori Caulfield, taught me how to grow into a woman through dancing. I learned about self-discipline, building a strong work ethic and always striving for my best. I was instilled with advice on healthy competition, how to take care of my body and how to manage my time efficiently. Each lesson pushed me to try new things, as I broke through my limitations and was urged to take more risks. Those aren't lessons you can teach a pre-teen easily.

Unfortunately, those lessons were temporarily disregarded as I became a teenager and started listening to outward messages instead of remembering what I had been taught. I soon became entangled in the dangerous world of an eating disorder, depending on bulimia more than on my own beliefs. My mind completely disassociated from my body and dancing became just another excuse to burn calories.

During those tumultuous teenage years, dance was both something I used to hurt my body and the only thing I could do to stay connected with it. After I recovered, dancing again became the joy it had once been. It reminded me of how precious my body was, and how to respect it. Most importantly, by reconnecting to myself through dance, I was able to save my own life.

***

It seems like a lifetime has elapsed since bulimia took control of me. After recovering, I dipped my toes in the film industry as an actor, worked many part time jobs and now travel all over the world in my career as a travel writer. My passion, though, has always brought me back to dance.

When the world hit the economic downturn in 2008, as a writer I had to find work in an industry where publications were letting go of staff at an alarming rate and long time newspapers were folding altogether. I wondered how I would survive.

I soon came up with the idea of researching traditional dances across Canada. What better way of combining my love of dance, my passion for travel and my curiosity for meeting new people than by going on the road of my favourite country and doing what makes me the happiest?

This book is a compilation of my travels across Canada: the stories I was told along the way, the individuals who inspired me with their resilience and the stunning backdrop that the country provided for my research.

When I learned what happened to our aboriginal people, though, I felt sick. I still feel sick. Although the stories that I heard about dancing don't even begin to contend with other more devastating accounts of abuse and trauma, they were overwhelming in their pain. I still don't fully comprehend what happened and I don't think enough Canadians take the time to reflect upon it.

Another part of me feels fortunate to have grown up in Canada. As a frequent traveller, I know how good most of us have it in this country, as imperfect as it is, and in this way I am proud to be Canadian for the choices that I have here and the freedoms that I take advantage of everyday.

So it is with this conflict that I give you this book. My hope when starting research on it almost four years ago was that I would cover as many different cultures as possible. Resources, of course, limited that ambitious goal, so I hope you will forgive me for leaving out so many important traditional dances that are alive in Canada. There are links at the end of the book for readers to share their own stories and cultures, and I hope that many will do so.

I began this project as a tribute to dance and I finish it as a love letter to Canada, one filled with celebrations and enthusiasm, as well as accusations and many questions.

Lori Henry
Vancouver, 2012

1 Nunavut: Banging on the Drum of History

Although the sun shines 20 hours a day, it is still cold underneath the big top tent. A massive heater chugs away near the stage, but most people seem oblivious to the chill that creeps inside their tuques and mittens. It is, after all, a bright summer evening. Children run around generating their own heat and families choose fold up chairs closest to the stage where they are saving spots for their friends. The evening show at the Alianait Arts Festival in Iqaluit is about to begin.

About 50 of us have taken our seats inside a purple and yellow striped big top tent for the evening performance by Artcirq, Nunavut's own circus group. It is my first time in Iqaluit, the capital city of this northern territory, and my first time seeing Artcirq perform live. As I have learned from my two previous trips up North, the territories are full of "first time" opportunities.

The young members of the Arctic's only circus, based in the remote community of Igloolik, make their way onto the stage dressed in white summer parkas and pants, some of the men going shirtless. The group doesn't wear exaggerated make up like most clowns do, but they delight in expressing their individual personalities through their movements and behaviour just like the more conventional red-nosed entertainers.

After showing off their juggling skills to much fanfare — two of them throwing bowling pins over the head of a third, who holds his in his mouth — a man in a polar bear costume enters stage left to stir up trouble. Not to be outdone, the group hams it up by contorting their faces in fear and eventually playing jokes on the bear in a tornado of playfulness, all the while two throat singers and drum dancers are providing a live soundtrack at the side of the stage.

Once the bear has retreated in defeat, the acrobats begin creating a human pyramid; perhaps trying to measure up to the size of the mighty bear, an animal the Inuit revere, having shared a home with it for thousands of years. One by one the nimble performers pile onto each other's shoulders, scrambling up thighs and outstretched arms.

With wide grins across their faces, five of them balance on each other. As the last one steps onto the back of his friend, he bends over so his hands rest less than a foot in front of him and completes the formation: creating a human *inuksuk*. The Inuit have used these rock navigational tools out on the land to mark travelling and hunting routes for generations, piling up stones and perching them on hilltops and ridges. In this human formation, each body represents a rock in a symbol of the ancient landmark.

After clambering down from each other's backs and shoulders, the group gets ready for another ancient tradition, a game called the high kick. Usually, this would be done with a wooden pole in an upside down "L," like the shape you draw when playing hangman, a piece of string dangling from the end. In this case, two of the acrobats transform into their own version of the pole by one standing on the other's shoulders.

The one on top pulls out a string with a target on the end (traditionally a piece of fur or bone) and dangles it down beside the competitor standing on the ground. As in the age-old Inuit game, the person competing has to run and jump, kicking one leg (or two in the two-foot high kick) high enough to touch the target. In this circus version, the one on top has the choice of making it easier or harder on the competitor, moving the target slightly up or down at his whim, much to the irritation of the one kicking, but much to the amusement of the rest of us.

Before Artcirq was formed, there were no such things as acrobats in Nunavut (the closest would be traditional Inuit games, as they include physicality and clowning, but certainly not what we see in modern circuses). Acrobatics came to the territory via Guillaume Saladin, originally from Quebec, who made annual summer trips north with his father during his childhood.

The idea began as workshops for Northern youth, where riding unicycles and juggling balls in Igloolik on ever-sunny summer days became a regular sight. This eventually led to Guillaume moving to the small Arctic community and founding Artcirq. Acrobatics, theatre, music and even some film provide youth with a creative outlet and, perhaps most importantly, something to do when the other option – getting into trouble – is all too tempting. Youth suicide in Inuit youth is 11 times higher than the rest of Canada, making projects like Artcirq so much more significant than just clowning around.

Although living in any rural area isolated from the rest of a country can be challenging, it was not always this way in the North. Challenging yes, but due to unsympathetic weather and a reliance on subsistence hunting; not because of drugs, alcohol, and crime. This pre-contact period was a test of survival between Inuit and the land, Inuit moving to the rhythm of the wildlife, believing in deities to help guide them along the tundra through hostile weather, and adapting their lifestyle to this climate.

Although some records indicate that European explorers found Canada's part of the Arctic thousands of years earlier, it was in the seventeenth century that waves of expeditions in search of a Northwest Passage began bringing hopeful explorers to Hudson Bay on a more regular basis. It would be these first collisions with European men that would eventually erode the ancient Inuit way of life.

Through the 18th and 19th centuries, explorers, followed by whalers and then missionaries, arrived on the rocky northern coasts. While they learned much from the aboriginal people about enduring the harsh environment, they also wanted to "improve" the Inuit by imposing European values and beliefs. Ancient ways were stifled, discouraged and then outright banned. The collision reverberated through the fibres of nomadic culture all over the North.

The most important belief of the Inuit was the one most feared by missionaries and the Canadian government – in the name of Arctic sovereignty and in their attempt to create their own version of how the Arctic should be – shamanism, one of the oldest belief systems on earth, was forbidden in an attempt to "civilize" the population. The children were forced out of their semi-nomadic existence and into residential schools, where their education left out survival skills and their own language, Inuktitut and similar tongues, in favour of things like Mathematics, English and Christianity.

Kiviuk, the Inuit creation story, tells the epic adventures of a shaman who battles through heroic feats and teaches a lesson in survival to all who hear his story. Nuliajuk (Sedna), the mother of all sea beasts, rules the underworld, her fingers cut off and turned into seals, whales and walruses. She controls the sea animals, so if her rules aren't obeyed, she will withhold these animals, the ones the Inuit need for survival.

These oral stories were told and re-told all over the Arctic (Kiviuq is found in different incarnations throughout Siberia, Alaska, Greenland and most Nordic countries) and form the core of Inuit history that is still passed on orally from one generation to the next. Other stories were told through dancing, often during the night through the long winter months.

Women would sit in a circle in a *qaggiq* (a winter gathering place or singing house) and begin singing, one of the men starting to dance. If no one wanted to start, sometimes a singer would begin a *pisiit* (personal song) and that man would be obligated to dance. The gathered group, consisting of the families who live in the area, would drink tea during occasional breaks but otherwise they danced and celebrated into the early morning, the women and children often joining in the dance near the end.

Drum dancing is thought to have come from shamanism. The gap in performing rituals when they were banned has lead to an irreversible cultural hole that Inuit are now working to refill, especially the younger generation that has grown up in a much more southern-influenced world than their parents and grandparents could have ever imagined. These days, drum dancing is really only performed at festivals and tourist events in an attempt to keep it alive.

***

On stage with Artcirq tonight is a young man in his early 20s named Dettrick Hala, part of a group called the Inuit Drum Dancers from the western community of Kugluktuk. He has been drum dancing since he was six years old and now performs all over the country. He is providing drum beats for the circus performance and then dancing solo. The rhythm from his drum reverberates through the cold tent; the ancient sound seems to come from the bowels of the earth. Wearing a black and white summer parka, matching pants and brown *kamiks* (cold weather boots), Dettrick holds the drum in his left hand, turning it from side to side and with a wooden stick in his right hand, he hits it underneath. His knees bounce softly and then his feet slowly shuffle from one foot to the other, keeping his own rhythm, swaying the back penguin-like tail of his parka from side to side, his head turning slightly from right to left with each beat. In a semi-hunched position, he travels gracefully around the stage in no particular pattern, letting the rhythm guide his breath, steps and tempo. At some point he yells out – a cry I feel in my gut – without missing a beat.

***

I wait for Dettrick the next day at the Elder's Centre, joining about 10 others for a workshop in drum dancing. Sitting nearby are two adorable girls, both about eight years old, and their mother; three young female volunteers for the festival; an older lady who is visiting from Montreal; a reporter from the Northern News Services; a local mother with her barely-walking daughter; and myself. Ironically, drum dancing was historically something men did.

Traditionally, at almost every gathering, whether it was a successful hunt, a boy's first kill, a celebration of life or honouring of death, a marriage, a change of season or the welcoming of visitors, drum dancing was a part of the occasion. As we all sit chatting with each other, I think of how we are all part of a celebration right now, gathered from different parts of the world here in Iqaluit for the Alianait festival, and that, sitting in an accidental (and a bit haphazard) circle, this is really a modern day reason to drum dance.

Although we're not sitting in a *qaggiq* warmed by a *qullik* (seal oil lamp), and the traditional way of inviting nearby settlements by word of mouth has been replaced by a snazzy website with email addresses, the idea of people travelling long distances to be here is still the same. (Of course, it is now summer, so instead of trudging along the snow-covered tundra with a dogsled team, people have taken an airplane or two to get here, as there are no roads connecting the communities in Nunavut to each other or to the south.)

Dettrick arrives half an hour late for the workshop, rushing in and apologizing for being behind schedule: he is still on his own time zone (Kugluktuk is two hours behind Iqaluit) and he simply slept in after performing last night.

Sleep is an interesting concept here during the summer. With the sun staying out for about 20 hours during the day at the end of June, when the Alianait festival takes place, darkness is a winter memory. I leave the big top tent every night after the evening show at about 9:00, sometimes after 11:00, and smile as I push open the tent flaps and find that the sun is still hanging around like a relentlessly energetic child who says, "Come plaaaayy with me!"

When I think of all the dances celebrating the sun that Canadian aboriginal people, and other cultures around the world, honour, I can better understand that tradition now, that relief and pleasure when the sun finally shines brightly in the spring and brings warmth and blooming vegetation to a needy climate. Most people down south have become so disconnected from the earth that we commemorate the changing of the seasons with new inventory in our favourite stores and blow out sales that keep us shopping for more.

Last summer I was in the Yukon, where the sun is just as dominant during the summer, and I remember standing at my window every night staring in bewilderment at the night sky, not wanting to sleep so I could save up some of the light and take it home with me – a solar powered woman.

In Iqaluit, I am staying with a sweet family who relocated here from Ottawa (and before that, Quebec) a few years ago, bringing up their now-seven-year-old son in Nunavut. The three of them live in a one-storey, three bedroom house in a "suburb" of the city. Down on the waterfront is a mishmash of houses that Inuit live in, along with amenities like the NorthMART (a big northern grocery-and-everything-else store), an "outdoors" store, Pizza Hut and a popular 24 hour eatery called, "The Snack." From there, the city is built up a hill along a few lengthy and winding streets, simple houses constructed up off the permafrost ground and all painted a different solid colour. Yards are strewn with appliances, children's toys and random debris, the ski-doos and winter gear packed away in underneath storage (or not).

My temporary home overlooks Koojesse Inlet, which belongs to Frobisher Bay. It is a wooden structure with a peaked roof but is otherwise a basic box shape. The outside has the standard red light facing the street, telling the water truck that stops by daily whether the house needs a refill, and a gravel front area for cars or trucks and snowmobiles in the winter. Inside is a family room with a TV and sewing machine table, kitchen, dining room and living room, and three bedrooms, all simply furnished with mismatching couches and chairs, and a scattering of toys. The walk-in pantry is filled with packaged food, a lot of it bought on visits down to Ottawa and brought back to dodge the doubled prices in the grocery stores here. My room is the tiny third bedroom, set up as a guest room with a single bed and bedside table. Although it's a basic house that feels more like an apartment, it costs them $4,000 per month in rent.

***

I'm not thinking about housing and rent as Dettrick rushes into the Elder's Centre and starts handing out drums. Almost the size of a small car tire, the instruments are bordered by light coloured wood and have a short handle to hold onto. Traditionally, these hand drums were used by hunters who were strong enough to hold the drums at torso height and keep a steady rhythm. Their drums were made from heavier wood and weighty caribou skins, much heftier than the ones we are practicing with today. But our version is still heavy enough for Dettrick to tell us with a knowing smile that "practicing makes it easier; your arm gets used to it."

I hope so. My mind starts racing with all the inane questions that immediately pop into my head: Are the muscles in your left arm (where he holds his drum) much stronger than your right? Do you do any exercises to balance them out? Have you ever tried holding the drum in your right hand, or do you always use your left?

These questions remind me of an earlier experience from two years ago while I was on an expedition cruise from northern Quebec up to Resolute Bay, sailing along the entire eastern coast of Baffin Island. One of the communities we stopped at was Pond Inlet, a gorgeous hamlet at the northern head of the island. I was sitting in a traditional sod house with an elder named Marta. She was gracious enough to chat and answer questions from ten eager visitors who had gathered around her in one of the oldest original houses in the community.

At one point someone asked Marta how long it took to boil water over the *qulliq* (a seal oil lamp used for, among other things, heating homes and, in the case of this sod house, as a sort of stove). The visitor wanted to compare the amount of time it took for a *qulliq* to do the job compared to our modern day kettles. Once the interpreter had translated, a soft look of amusement settled on Marta's face. She looked at the person asking the question and said simply, "Until it's finished, but who really knows? It's pretty fast." Then her face scrunched into a wrinkled smile and she giggled at the absurdity of measuring time so closely. What does it matter, really, how long a task like that takes?

***

In learning disciplines like ballet and jazz, students learn by memorizing positions and striving to perfect them in every class. Not so much with drum dancing. There is certainly coordination needed between your feet and your arms, but there isn't a set of steps you have to master and put together in a combination. Beating the drum is like a musician whose guitar becomes part of his hands or a ballerina whose point shoes are extensions of her feet; the drum must become an appendage of your arm.

Although this workshop is to teach us how to drum dance, the concept of learning in a classroom-like setting is a new way of doing things for the Inuit. Children used to watch their parents and grandparents dance during celebrations, probably not conscious that they were learning anything at all. But as they got older, they instinctively knew how to dance and could join in without missing a beat.

That's the approach I take here, just sped up a few years: I have been watching drum dancing for the last three days and hope that the movement has somehow sunken in without me knowing. I watch Dettrick lean in and out of each beat, almost mirroring in the rest of his body how his right arm is lightly pounding on the side of the drum; I notice his feet shuffle in a step-together-step-together pattern, knees bending fluidly, while his upper body almost protects the drum by slightly curving over it.

I think of all these things as I beat my drum and try to move in a similar way to him. I hold my drum in my left hand, swaying it back and forth so I can hit one side of the circular wooden part, and then the other. Once I stop thinking, though, and the group naturally falls onto the same beat, I can feel my body relax into the movements and start yielding to the swaying motion. The deep pounding of the drum thuds inside my core and the physical vibrations from the wood join the sound there. I am drum dancing.

Dettrick wraps up the workshop by introducing an old competition, one he has only heard about from hearsay, but one that would surely have kept families entertained in past generations. He brings out a "really, really old hat" that was made by an Inuit woman who was probably over a hundred years old. She gathered various animal skins, over the course of several hunting seasons to create this durable piece.

"I think I'm going to put it down after this trip," Dettrick confides, staring at it sadly. "I've had this ever since the start of our practices for the [Vancouver] Olympics. It was given to me from my [drum dancing] group."

Like a *tuque* that has flaps reaching down below the ears, this finely stitched garment has a dark brown centre made from some sort of bird feathers, with the beak still attached and jutting out of the forehead, strips of short-haired, lighter brown fur and silky white fur at the crown and along the outer edges. The white fur is that of the weasel, caught during the winter season when their pelts are white.

Hanging from the beak is a piece of weasel fur that forms the crux of the contest: the competitor puts on the hat, weasel dangling from the front, and must spin it around and around like a head banger at a heavy metal concert by circling his head without letting the weasel waver and touch the hat. A drum dancer provides the beat that the competitor must move to, timing his head to the rhythm. "To keep the beat, just watch the drummer's feet," Dettrick instructs us.

After watching his demonstration, I volunteer to give it a try and everyone forms a circle around me. Walking to the centre, Dettrick places the exquisite hat in my hands and I am surprised at how soft the fur is, expecting it to have degraded in some way over the years. But the only sign of age is in the small tears along the seams that hold the furs together, now threatening to split.

I gingerly place the hat on my head – down south we would lock this up behind glass in a museum, giving it special lighting and a specific humidity and temperature – and get into position. With my legs spread out just wider than my shoulders, knees bent and hands resting on my thighs, Dettrick starts hitting his drum. Around and around my head twirls to get that little weasel circling, my legs bouncing me up and down until I am almost jumping and quite dizzy. I have no idea if the weasel ever does touch the hat, but I finish when I am out of breath, a bit light-headed and giggling at how fun it was. I'm sure in past times, winners were chosen arbitrarily by those watching and would have been hotly contested, adding to the enjoyment of the game.

As with other oral cultures, it can be difficult to know where a game like this came from and how much it has changed from generation to generation. I found this particularly true with drum dancing, as some Inuit are hesitant to believe it was actually done. I chatted with John Houston about this, someone who has seen engravings and etchings, as well as more recent photos from the early 1900s, showing Inuit drum dancing.

John was born in Cape Dorset to the notable artist, author, designer and filmmaker James Houston, and educator Alma Houston, who are originally from the south but spent much of their time in the North working with Inuit communities. James is particularly beloved for initiating the development of Inuit art sales in the south, as well as introducing printmaking to the Inuit. The New York Times referred to James as being "almost single-handedly responsible for introducing contemporary Eskimo art to an international audience."

His son John followed suit by returning to the North in his adult years to fill the Art Advisor position for the Pangnirtung Co-operative's printmaking project in the small hamlet of Pangnirtung, which has now expanded its printmaking venture into a self-supporting arts centre of weavers, sewers, sculptors and drawers. John is also a filmmaker, his films telling some of the most important oral Inuit stories.

I met John in 2008 aboard an expedition cruise with a company called Adventure Canada. They run Arctic (and other) voyages and often invite

John aboard to lead talks about Inuit culture and to share his knowledge of the North with passengers. Because he speaks Inuktitut, he has been able to learn a lot from the elders, including why some Inuit might not believe the ancient stories or even in drum dancing itself.

"There are some people in the Arctic who would just like to say that none of that ever happened," John shakes his head. "There's been a sort of a brainwashing afoot because, otherwise, why would a young person not know all that? That would be all common knowledge within the culture, if there hadn't been an extensive attempt to wipe it out. But I say, 'Why? How is it going to hurt humanity for people to have music? How is it going to hurt humanity for people to dance?' I don't understand it and I don't accept it."

In the late 1950s, international attention became focussed on what was being portrayed as the starving, deprived Inuit, then called Eskimo, in Canada's North. The Canadian government moved into action by doing something about the "problem" that was tarnishing this country's reputation: they introduced resettlement.

The government descended on the vast Arctic to round up the semi-nomadic families, many of whom had already transitioned from their fully nomadic lifestyles to ones conducive to trading with the newly-arrived whalers, and put them into what are now 25 communities spread over Nunavut (at that time, the Northwest Territories). The Inuit were given health care, a new education system and food; best of all, Canada could now count the population, track them and report internationally on how their Northern people were "progressing" into a "civilized" population.

Incredulously, in this quest to gain control over the North, Inuit were dispatched from the land where their ancestors had taught them to hunt and survive, to areas completely foreign to them. By displacing hundreds of families, it enhanced Canada's sovereignty in the North. As our Prime Minister Stephen Harper is fond of saying, you have to use it or lose it.

When the government said they would take all the children and relocate them to centralized schools to give them a "real" education, the parents and grandparents were confused. This is a culture where people rely on each other for survival, where interdependence isn't a nice sentiment, but a necessity. You can't just take the children away and re-educate them without crippling the whole societal dynamic. So the older generation said, well, if the children are being taken away, we'll go with them.

John said that his mother, the late Alma Houston, was one of the ones who wanted to help the Inuit stay where they were, out on the land. She realized this lack of cultural understanding right away. An educator herself, she cited the fly-in doctors in other parts of the world and said that she would set up a sort of mobile classroom, travelling through the Inuit camps along the southern Baffin coast and teach them the things that were on the curriculum. At least in this way, families could stay together and their lifestyles wouldn't be so drastically interrupted.

"You don't have to move them," said John, quoting his mother. "They can stay close to nature, they can have their elders around them, keep that system that's been working and has allowed them to survive – I mean, it's the harshest test of whether a culture is working or not. I don't think there's any harsher proving ground than the Arctic, so obviously they have something that's working. So instead of busting that all up and trying to reinvent the wheel, how about letting them have all of that and we'll just add: you want them to be able to speak X level of English? We'll do that. You want a certain amount of math? Okay, we'll add that. We can do all that, we can have mobile classrooms."

But the government would have none of it. They had made up their minds and relocations would be happening. This changed the Inuit lifestyle as drastically as it could have been changed, and at a speed that didn't allow them much time to adapt.

John remembers going to school at the newly-formed communities: "We would bundle up and go off to school, which was a one-room schoolhouse. The building (nobody ever throws away buildings up there) has since been used variously as a post office, a sewing centre, and I think part of it's now a bed and breakfast. We would go and sit in there and you'd have to get there early enough in the morning. If you weren't there on time, then you didn't get the rations that they doled out. I know they didn't call it Health Canada at the time, but they'd give you one of those melmac cups full of cocoa and you got a black gelatine capsule of vitamins, you got a white powdery pill, and you had to take all that. If you didn't get there in time for that, you weren't allowed to go to school, so you'd just get sent home…

"I find myself wondering today what great stuff, like we had our See Dick and Jane and See Spot Run books and *that* was our bid to replace the age old knowledge of the elders? They were of course deemed unqualified to teach the kids because they didn't have paper certificates. I grew up in the middle of all that stuff."

Surprisingly, while onboard an Adventure Canada cruise, John was telling this same story to a passenger, whose eyes widened more and more while he spoke. She said, "Well, let me tell you, your mother wasn't alone."

"This woman said she had been in health care," John paraphrases, "and she had been up on the northern tip of Baffin Island. She said when the government tried to bring in their health system, which was the same idea as pulling everybody all together so you can just administer them more easily. It's really just a people moving issue: don't stop to think about the dreams and goals of the people, but just look at it like you're going to build a little town, with little blocks, and you just say, 'Well, let's take all these people and haul them in here and haul them in there and never mind consultation.' Apparently she was also very vocal about that at the time, she was just outraged at the way that it was being handled and spoke up, and she was told the identical message as my mother, that there could be no dissenting voices and she should shut up now because they'd already made up their minds."

Probably the most well-known story of relocation is that of John Amagoalik, considered one of the founding fathers of Nunavut and affectionately called John A. by Nunavummiut. His family and others were relocated from Nunavik in northern Quebec to what is now Resolute Bay and Grise Fiord in the High Arctic (the two most northern communities in Canada), completely different environments from where they came from: here the sun doesn't set in the summer and the winter has uninterrupted months of darkness. Wildlife patterns for hunting were completely unknown to them and the entire landscape that they now had to make a living from was an alien place. These Inuit were dropped off on the beach without anything, apparently only given a few old buffalo and caribou hides, and expected to make a new home on the assumption that they would know how to survive anywhere in the North.

John Houston believes that the Inuit survived relocation in spite of the hardships, not because the government succeeded in their plan to "improve" the Inuit.

"I don't think that our culture, our non-native culture, can really chalk, let's say John Amagoalik, up as a win for our side, to point at him and say, 'Well, look, there's a very articulate man.' I've seen him as a public speaker, and he's very impressive, one of a group of highly articulate Inuit. We might tend to look at them and say, 'Well, see, look at them, we did good.' And I'd have to say that we did bad. I don't think that we did good. I think that the fact that those Inuit of that time are as articulate as they are and as able to cope with the rapid changes, is a testament to a long time Inuit genius for adapting, for thinking on their feet and adapting to change, in this case, in a hostile situation."

Along with most of their other traditions, dancing, once an integral part of the Inuit culture, was almost wiped out. Because the missionaries' main focus was on introducing Christian values to the Inuit in their new lives, they cut the cord on ancient wisdom and beliefs; they disallowed the rituals and festivals that the Inuit had celebrated since their beginning.

One fascinating dance (and one which two of John Houston's late friends re-enacted for his film *Nuliajuk: Mother of the Sea Beasts*) is the Mad Dance of Qailertetang, part of the fall Sedna festival. Also called Nuliajuk, and many other names, Sedna is one of the most feared deities who lives under the sea and controls all of the sea animals. This dance was best recorded in writing by German explorer and anthropologist Franz Boas in 1888.

During Franz's travels through Baffin Island in the 19th century, he witnessed a Sedna festival near Cumberland Sound. Two cloaked people dressed in sealskin masks, a woman's "overjacket," several pairs of breeches and heavy boots, would interrupt the festival and begin whirling around and around. They would have floats made of sealskin (that was attached to a hunter's harpoon) hanging from their backs and blown up with air.

These masked people, probably shamans embodying Sedna's representatives (*qailertetang*), would be so heavily dressed that their sex couldn't be distinguished. They would start pointing to men and women, who would recoil in fear. Each of the pairs would then become ritualistically married for a period of time, maybe even a few days. Franz writes that "these pairs run, pursued by the *qailertetang*, to the hut of the woman, where they are for the following day and night man and wife."

Then all the men "attack" the *qailertetang* as if stabbing them with spears and knives, hitting them and jumping on their backs as they "kill" them. Eventually, the floats on their backs are broken open to symbolize the killing and everyone collapses on the ground in exhaustion. This is the end of the dance, the *qailertetang* has been spiritually reborn and they slowly recover from the ritual. This is the time when the Inuit can ask the questions they most need an answer to, usually predictions about future hunts and other events that may happen. These life changing questions are answered in murmurs that the person asking has to interpret for themselves.

John was told by his two friends who re-enacted the Mad Dance of Qailertetang for him, that, even after the missionaries arrived and tried to eliminate Inuit rituals, "The Mad Dance of Qailertetang was still being performed," he continues, "but in secret, when they were young on Blacklead Island. Missionary Reverend Edmund James Peck, an Anglican missionary, was there at that time. There were Inuit children spies who would pull up the edge of the tent or peek in the window. I believe he was in, for significant parts of the year, a framed building. So they would peek in the window and they would ascertain that he had gone to sleep. Apparently he snored rather loudly, this old patriarchal, great big long flowing bearded missionary, and when they heard his snoring then they would give signal or they would run and tell the Inuit population, who *needed* to do these various rites and rituals because at that time the missionaries hadn't yet broken their direct connection with the mother of the sea beasts, and they had to still keep obeying Her rules."

The late Cornelius Nutaraq, an elder from Pond Inlet, said, "When the Faith [Christianity] came, we confessed and converted. The missionaries said our old ways must be abandoned, including any storytelling to do with shamanism, and drum dancing and singing. All these things were to be discarded, but it turns out some things necessary for today were thrown out with the rest."

Cornelius was speaking to John Houston in 2004, who filmed the interview, and it mirrored what John told me: "If that's your culture, that's who you are and that's how you relate to the world and if somebody summarily says that they want to, without asking you, but just telling you, they want to remove all that, wipe it all out, it's not without repercussions. Inuit can adapt and Inuit can survive, but it's not without repercussions…"

But "Bendo Schmidt, the woman who portrays Nuliajuk in my second film," John resumes, "told me she does not see these things as thrown away. She doesn't believe they can be, and tells aboriginal youth that all the white man can do is stuff traditional Inuit culture in a suitcase, and hide it under the bed. For those who would care to try, it is a matter of throwing off the covers, digging under the bed, pulling out the suitcase, opening it, and taking back the things Inuit need most to move forward."

Those repercussions are the problems facing modern Inuit today, things like youth suicide, alcoholism, drug use, crime and depression. These teenagers might leave their house in the morning on dog sled, going out on a bowhead whale hunt, maybe building and sleeping in an igloo overnight, coming home with a catch from their harpoon, and then sitting down at the computer to catch up with their activity feed on Facebook and watch their favourite videos on YouTube. This is the sort of dual life that young people are trying to work their way through, a clash of ancient traditions and a world that has no time for those customs.

As John says, "It happened in such a short period of time and I think it's hard for anyone to really understand that, if it hasn't all happened to you, just like a tsunami, I think. And it's still going on. It's the 500 channel universe and today I guess the struggle is for Inuit to find themselves in it, to look at that maelstrom of data that's coming at them sideways, and to say, 'Where am I in all this? What's going to be my future?' And I don't pretend to have any answers for that but I think all good people should be asking that question and saying, 'Let's not go half way and just dump a whole lot of stuff on Inuit and then wait and see what happens.'"

Thankfully, all was not lost. Although not a part of everyday life anymore, drum dancing still happens at celebrations, festivals, special occasions and for tourists; people are researching documents and photos to understand the traditions and, most importantly, asking the elders to remember what used to be. Some elders don't want to remember, others have a hard time remembering, but as they begin to pass away from old age, their memories are all the Inuit have to connect them with their past.

***

It is the first time I have heard throat singing live. Maria Illungiayok and Lois Suluk-Locke take the stage, somewhat shyly, after Dettrick finishes his drum dancing performance. Both of their faces shine with pleasure and they look out at the audience playfully. Maria's *amauti*, a parka designed to hold a baby in the back pouch, is black with a white border around it and along the sleeves, white fringe hanging from the penguin-like back and around to the front; Lois' is white with yellow and blue horizontal lines and diamond-shaped designs on the hood. Each of them wears a thin headband with strips of coloured fabric dangling down the sides of their faces.

Linking their forearms together, they stand face to face preparing for competition. Maria starts the song with a low, guttural sound from the bottom of her throat, an imitation of an animal or a sound that evokes something specific in the story they're telling, and Lois repeats the sound, alternating back and forth and sometimes overlapping their voices as the pace picks up.

The women sway back and forth from foot to foot, shifting their weight in a kind of dance as they hold onto a microphone in the middle of them so that the whole tent can hear their song. Each woman's pitch and sound is different and their guttural voices, alternating with deep inhales as they gather air, creates a melody that sounds like a rushing river, a dog team running or even a saw cutting back and forth, depending on the song.

As Maria tries to trick Lois by changing the tempo and picking up speed, the rhythm becomes intense and their breathing gets heavier. And then, without warning, they both start giggling hysterically and let go of each other, the audience clapping their approval.

In a throat singing workshop the next day, I learn that Maria and Lois are from the community of Arviat, the southernmost settlement in Nunavut on the Hudson Bay near the Manitoba border, and they have shared throat singing at festivals in Dublin, Mexico and Santa Fe, sometimes being the first Inuuk the country has ever seen.

Throat singing, like drum dancing, is as old as anyone can remember. "Throat singing was a form of chanting in worship," Lois explains to the group. "Today we throat sing for entertainment, good competition and use it as an identity of being an Inuk woman… We also do some traditional singing and each song is the composer's experience. They're usually experiences of their hunting trip or a form of celebration and each person can give that song to their namesake. So some songs may be really old… We don't have anything written down of how old the songs are. They might have changed just a little bit, but these songs could be at least a few thousand years old."

Traditionally, two women would stand almost mouth to mouth, but today it's more common for throat singers to just clasp forearms and face each other. Elders may do things more traditionally, but it all depends. I was told that elders sound very different than those from younger generations, "like they're saying words" as they sing. Lois says that the elders sound like old maids. "I can't wait to sound like an old maid! The throat singing would be much more rich, I think."

As with drum dancing, throat singing was not allowed once Christianity was introduced. "In the 40s or 50s, the church tried to ban the throat singing," says Lois quietly. "Because that happened, my mother does not know how to throat sing, but my grandmother does. And now we're claiming it back and saying it wasn't right for someone to tell us not to do what we use as entertainment, chanting, worship and good competition."

Now, throat singing is being carried on by women like Maria and Lois, as well as being re-defined by solo artists like Tanya Tagaq, who is mixing traditional sounds with modern beats, instruments and English vocals. (Tanya has also worked with artists like Icelandic Bjork and the Kronos Quartet to create stunning work.)

Competitions, almost always between women, are like the last one standing: whoever can last the longest in a song without breaking the rhythm (usually by laughing), is the winner. And with the breath, probably the most important part of singing, forming an almost panting sound on the inhale and an animal-like growl on the exhale, combined with the close connection to the other woman, laughing is inevitable. When I try during the workshop, not only can I not produce a rich growl from my throat muscles (it is more like Kermit the Frog), but I am making myself dizzy and giddy by breathing so quickly.

Even with the tiring action of using the throat so directly, Maria and Lois demonstrate many songs for us (sometimes with the accompaniment of drummers who are hanging around), from the most basic song to one about being happy to have woken up to another day after a successful hunt; from a puppy trying to keep up with a dog team and a river that rushes and swells, to a saw (that sounds exactly like a saw!) and ones called "The Love Song" and "The Mosquito."

The sensuality of the songs, because the singing comes from so deep within the stomach and lungs, then the throat and breath, is primal; I can feel it resonating in my own stomach and through my body, the intimacy created by the singers drawing listeners deep into their melodies.

As much as the songs don't change (Lois likens it to "trying to re-word the Happy Birthday song, you can't do it"), and they vary as the dialects of Inuktitut do across Nunavut, there are composers and young people taking an interest in bringing back the old traditions, with their own generational influence.

One volunteer at the festival who was at the throat singing workshop told us that once, while she was teaching "The Mosquito" song to a group in Ottawa, she decided to split them into two groups, one group learning the lead sound in one room, the other learning the following sound in another room. Because there are two distinct parts to this song (in most songs, the person following must repeat the same sound the leader makes, which can lead to a cat and mouse chase as the lead tries to throw the other woman off), each group learned their different "part." The two groups were then brought into the same room and sang the song together. She said it was crazy. And completely contemporary.

***

For all the things that Maria and Lois teach us about throat singing, they are still as curious about other cultures as those of us taking their workshop are about theirs. Lois ends the session by saying, "If there aren't any other questions, I really want to go to the Greenlandic workshop."

This is the fourth out of five workshops going on today as part of the festival. Earlier, preschool children learned basic music, there were the Inuit drum dancing and throat singing workshops that I went to, and now there is a Greenlandic folk dance and mask dance workshop.

Most of us follow her from the Elder's Centre across the street to the Nakasuk Elementary School gym, a rectangular bunker-like building with tiny porthole windows that look like peeping holes from a mother ship. Inside, a group of Greenlandic dancers from Nuuk called Nuummi Alikkusersuisartut Isiginnaartitsisartullu Peqatigiffiat (or NAIP) are getting ready to teach us their traditional folk dancing.

The Nunavummiut are excited to learn some Greenlandic dance, as it is similar to the set dancing that the European whalers brought to their own territory. It has been carried on in almost all of the communities up here, especially in the winter when there are many evening dances. The tips of Greenland and Nunavut can almost kiss each other at the northern ends of the land, making these two cultures very similar. Each one has their own style and steps, but each uses the fiddle and accordion to play the reels and jigs of old time Europe.

The clothing is the biggest difference. The women from Greenland wear exquisitely beaded shawls of reds, blues, yellow and white, all patterned in their own way, with different shades of red long sleeved shirts underneath; sashes wrap around their waists in varying designs, equally as colourful. Brown fur shorts are brightened up with thick vertical bands of red and white at the front. One more band of bright flower-patterned fabric sits on top of white boots. In contrast, the men wear simple white, long sleeved hooded shirts (*annoraaq*), black pants and black sealskin boots with a thin silver band of sealskin around them.

During the group's evening performance the night before, they danced a few different sets to pre-recorded fiddle music, smiling and laughing as they threaded through and around eight hand reel-like formations. The men would do footwork in between travelling steps, not unlike step dancing, but more of a shuffle with their feet that bordered on stomping, while the women calmly shuffled from foot to foot.

We jump right into it at the workshop, the team of eight Greenlandic dancers teaching us short phrases of each set at a time. We're usually pretty good until we have to change partners by weaving through each other and then returning to our original partner. Mostly people are just laughing and trying their best not to bump into each other.

This kind of folk dance was introduced by the whalers, just as it had been in Canada's North, and just like Canada's northern aboriginal people, Greenlanders believed in deities and spirits. So after their folk dance performance last night, the group transformed themselves for an older traditional dance, the Greenlandic mask dance. Tukummeq and Valerie, two of the female dancers, came back out on stage with five male members of Artcirq. Two of them drummed at the side of the stage, but the other three were unrecognizable: they had painted their faces completely black with red and white lines covering their cheeks, chin and forehead.

I would learn later that these colours represent important aspects of *uaajeerneq*, the mask dance. Black represents strength, spirits, the unseen and good powers; red represents life, the blood that runs through their veins and fertility; and white represents the bones of their ancestors, so they will always remember and honour where they came from.

Along with black faces, Tukummeq and Valerie were also wearing black, long sleeved leotards, which represented them being naked. They had become *toornaq*, which are spirits, and spirits, well, don't wear clothing. So the women had on small fur loincloths to cover their *eetup* (no translation needed), while the men were bare-chested, with white long shorts.

As they entered the stage, making monkey-like noises and looking out at the audience in curiosity, they began stepping down the stage stairs and into the crowd. The children at the front were giggling half hysterically, half frightened, at these masked performers that they thought they might, maybe have recognized. The dancer's movements were animalistic and scary, sexual, funny and cute, all done purposefully to encompass the spirit they were representing. Each of them had an animal that formed the basis of their movements, which changed depending on how they were feeling or what was going on in their life.

Tukummeq said that during her time in Iqaluit, her animal was a bird, so that affected the way she used her arms and legs, where her centre of gravity was, and the sounds and voices that she used.

As they made their way through the aisles under the tent, children were reaching their hands out to touch them and then running away squealing, others were hiding behind their parents or an older child; adults were staring incredulously as the performers got up close and personal to try to elicit reactions from the crowd.

As the dancers got closer to me, I noticed that they all had two small round circles jutting out from each side of their chins, just below their lower lips. It gave them a warrior-like look. This is actually a stick with two balls attached to the ends that the dancers put on their lower gums inside their mouths. Like two white gumballs or mini dumbbells jutting out of their lower cheeks, it symbolizes testicles for the fertility component of the dance. A lot of Vaseline must be used so the stick and balls don't rub painfully into their cheeks.

After the folk dancing workshop today, the adults clear to the side of the gym and the children (plus me and two other adults) eagerly gather around Tukummeq. She is about to teach us how to do the mask dance and how to apply the mask, so we all sit cross legged, scattered around the centre of the floor where Tukummeq is squished in the middle with her make up and mirror.

She begins to use the black paint to cover her face, make up she bought from the store. Her ancestors would have used "face paint" made from sod and blood, which would have scared the children even more.

"So, how did you like the performance?" she asks the children.

"You were creepy."

"You were scary."

"My friend touched one of the guys!"

"My sister was totally scared of you."

"Good," Tukummeq says in her soft, maternal voice. The *uaajeerneq* is danced by *toornaq* to help, especially children, deal with their fears so they know that it is okay to be afraid. It was often performed during the long, dark winters when there was less abundance of food and it was harder to keep their spirits up without sunlight. *Uaajeerneq* was common in Greenland because it was so important to raise strong children who could survive the northern climate.

"In the old times it was very important that the kids should be tough," says Tukummeq, "because if the kids were not tough, they would be weak as adults and would not be able to give food, if they're boys. If he's weak, he probably won't be able to give food to his family, so he won't be of any help. Always the survival of the fittest, that was so true back then.

"For example, east and west Greenlanders use kayaks to hunt, so it's important that the kids, as babies, learn not to be afraid of the water. So the father would take his son in a small kayak – maybe two or three years old – and go out in the cold water in the summer or winter and turn the kid around so he faces death [plunges him into the water]. So the first time the father does that, he'll pull him back up when the boy starts to move a lot. The second time, he takes him up when he's not moving anymore. And that means that the boy understands that he should not be afraid of the water. If he's able to turn around and get up again by himself with the kayak, go in the water and up again, he'll survive even the worst storms in the water."

After Tukummeq has applied her mask, we are invited to get up and try the dance for ourselves. She leads us through slow movements where we follow her basic motions, and then must branch out to find our own animal.

I'm not sure if it's because I immediately thought of a monkey when I saw the *uaajeerneq* performed, but I am feeling particularly monkey-like. So my arms circle in with my fingers in my armpits, and my legs feel a bit bow legged as I make my way around the gym floor. My head starts to cock from one side to the other mischievously, laughing along with the rest of the group.

One look at the children and their serious immersion in their characters, though, and I decide to just go for it. I make my way closer to the centre of our motley crew and dig deeper into the movements. My knees bend more intensely and my centre of gravity lowers, walking more nimbly. It takes me back to theatre school where I trained as an actor and didn't judge the strange things the teachers asked me to do, like walking while leading with my right hip bone or doing a scene without words by only conversing in sounds ranging from guttural to high pitched. I just went with it.

Tukummeq starts to make noises and tells us to let out the voice of our animal. It's like a jungle in here. I can't re-create the sounds that came out of my mouth now, nor do I want to, but I join the symphony of wild clamouring; I am a monkey spirit, after all. Chirping birds and gnarly polar bears become the norm in this gym.

There is something refreshing about joining a group of children, especially the wild Inuit children who grow up without the same strict rules that we have in the south, and remember how to be free again. Here, the land is always the third partner in the dance, the other character in the play, the third winger in the hockey game, but it makes up the biggest part of their life. The Inuit never considered their land to be stark, empty and desolate until we told them it was.

When John Houston talks about his childhood in Cape Dorset, he laughs at the misconception that the North is a barren, boring place.

"There were endless things to do. People sometimes say, 'Well, what would you *do* up there?' thinking of it as something so remote and austere, but the days were packed. We used to go sliding: my brother and I and most of the Inuit at the time had these furs that had been custom tailored for us by some of the local sewers – who were among the world's greatest sewers, I would imagine – I mean, to take two pieces of seal skin and sew them, lap them like this [he shows me by overlapping his fingers] and sew them together so they dry when they're pulled together and become waterproof, it's pretty phenomenal. You could walk around in the water with those like rubber boots. Of course, it's a life or death thing: if your stitches weren't quite right and if that person's feet got soaked in the middle of winter, then they might be a goner.

"All of those kinds of skills were very much in practice and when we went sliding, we had a layer of underwear, which was the caribou skin of August, a finer, thinner skin, shorter hairs. Over that, with a suitable air space in between, we had a second full caribou layer with the hair facing out. We had twice the insulation that the caribou themselves had, for goodness sakes. So there we were, and we had other skins like polar bear skins and seal skins, and we'd go off on the *kinngait*, these hilltops or small mountains around the community – it took forever to get ourselves up there – and then we would slide down pell mell on these furs and we would hit a rock or something and go rolling crazily out of control and then just lie there in the snow laughing.

"People always talk about the Arctic and the freezing cold. Oh yeah, it was cold… but I don't really remember that. I remember the times that I was overheated; I remember some times when I thought I was going to faint or pass out or die from the heat."

These kinds of stories make me smile because they seem so contradictory to what we think the North is. I have only been to Canada's territories three times, and what I've learned is that for every assumption southerners have, there are countless stories like this one that turn our ideas of the North upside down. And that's one of the reasons that the territories are so special: we can't begin to imagine what it's like to live there and what it was like to make a living before European contact changed the lifestyle so dramatically.

I hope, with the introduction of fast food chains in Nunavut (the first Tim Hortons arrived in Iqaluit at the end of 2010) and the pursuit by some Nunavummiut to have the same conveniences that we have down south, the Inuit never forget how special their home is. The rituals and celebrations that kept them warm, the ingenious hunting techniques that kept them fed and the oral stories that passed down this knowledge were taken away from them, temporarily. As they struggle to remember and to work through their painful recollections, I hope the damage will eventually heal and they can reclaim their past. In fact, they are already in the process of reclaiming it.

They must also forge their way forward. With the harsh climate they have lived in for thousands of years as their training, is it any wonder they are slowly finding ways to adapt and recover what was lost? Although there have been massive obstacles, and there will surely be many more, how can we doubt their strength and resiliency?

Nunavut, after all, means "our land" in Inuktitut and even though they have been introduced to a whole new way of living, I hope the next generation will never forget how their ancestors survived pre-contact. I hope the land will always remain theirs. It is now our turn to listen and learn from them.

CANADA

NEWFOUNDLAND

Cape
Breton

NOVA
SCOTIA

USA

2 Nova Scotia: Stepping through Cape Breton Island

I have been in Cape Breton for three days and it already feels like home. The video playing on the TV in front of me at the Gaelic College of Celtic Arts and Crafts tells me that there are really only two places in the world: Cape Breton and… away. I'm starting to believe that.

I had heard snippets of talk all day about the dance tonight, as people arranged car pools and set times to meet each other. I had run into two step dancers, young women who go to university in the province, and who invited me to tag along with them to a family square dance, something I "shouldn't miss."

They pick me up with another girl and we stop at a run down gas station that looks like it hasn't been cared for in a few decades. We squish together in the back seat to fit in one of their guy friends, who is leaving his car here and riding with us. We're heading to Glencoe Mills, a miniscule community in Inverness County between Whycocomagh and Port Hood, the scene of a long-standing Thursday night square dance in the parish hall.

We had left from Iona, near the centre of the island, and have travelled west along the main road (one of two options), taking a ferry to cross over the tail end of the St. Andrews Channel and into Whycocomagh. Just past town is an unmarked turn off, the one we are searching for, and we descend into complete darkness.

It's already 10:00 pm and the dirt road that has now become our link to Glencoe is encased by forest on both sides, lit only by our high beams. As the streetlights from the main road get farther away from us, we drive slowly through the one and a half lane road in between a forest that looks like it could grow in and swallow us at any moment.

My first plan upon hearing of the dance was to drive there on my own. Who do I know in Cape Breton? I was given oral directions like "it should be the second left" and "there might be a sign on the road, but it doesn't have a name," and was then printed out a Google Map. Of course, none of the country roads are even on Google's radar, so there were hand drawn lines with landmark hints written beside them and arrows pointing to general spots. Everyone just knows how to get there – and if you're coming from anywhere else on the island, Glencoe is just off the main highway – but from Iona it gets challenging.

Inside the country roads, there are a couple of forks we have to choose from, instinct taking over on which way to go. My fellow car mates have been going to the Glencoe dance since they were children, so it's a matter of navigating through their faded memories to find the hall from this direction in such darkness. I am so glad I'm not driving alone, as I would most surely have turned around by now and reluctantly gone back to my empty hotel room.

After what seems like an hour on the dirt road, we finally detect light up ahead and the sound of a fiddle escaping through cracks in the closed doors. Young people are hanging out on the grass around the building, drinking beer stashed in the trunks of their cars; dancers are coming in and out of the front door to join in on the fun and then cool down from the heat inside.

We eagerly unload ourselves from the confines of the car, happy to get back outside to the warm summer night. I'm introduced to almost everyone outside as we gradually make our way towards the hall. Every time the front door opens, a whiff of a fiddle tune and musical feet escape the building and fill the black night with life. I follow the other four into the entryway where a middle aged woman collects $6 from each of us and puts a stamp on all of our hands.

The hall is already in full swing, with half of the crowd resting on benches around the perimeter and the other half twirling their partners in the middle. I am immediately swept into another era when family dances were marked on social calendars with anticipation and whole towns came together to spend the night revelling.

As a city girl, I often forget how small towns retain that charming old world feeling of kinship that gets lost when skyscrapers and office towers block so much human interaction. Here, they're not divided by buildings, although I guess small town gossip can be just as dividing, but Cape Breton Island is like one big small town. You might find yourself driving for an hour to get to a dance, but if it's billed as a good one (usually by who the fiddlers are), then you'll see the same people from all over the island there.

I take a quick scan around the room at the smiling dancers in the centre, the sweating folks sitting down for a rest on the periphery, and a few of the older generation tending to the home baked goods and water being sold from a simple concession to my left. In front of me a young girl of about nine links arms with her grandfather and they gallop around the floor to get back to their position in the set.

Stashing my purse underneath the bench just to the left of the entrance, the current square set comes to an end and those sitting on the sidelines get ready to jump into the action. As if on cue, I hear my name, in a place where I only know the four people I came to the dance with, and look up to a smiling man in his 60s drenched in sweat.

"I was told to get you up on the dance floor," he says, offering me his arm. How can I refuse?

Burton MacIntyre is a force of nature. His thinned white hair and knee replacement surgeries don't dampen his spirit to dance at all. In fact, I'm sure he can out dance anyone in this room, which we do together until after 1:00 the next morning.

I learn the sets here by trial and error, allowing Burton to guide me in the right direction, in and out of the many partners who are doing the same thing. He yells out often, Gaelic cries that release his enthusiasm and enjoyment, and I can't stop the smile from swelling on my face: am I infecting the rest of the hall or are their smiles infecting me? It doesn't leave my face the entire night, only taking a break every now and then as I catch my breath.

Some of the younger women are excellent step dancers and keep it up during the setting steps of the squares. This is the old Highland way of dancing, a way many want to keep up. At the end of the 19th century, quadrilles became the popular dance of choice, so many dancers stopped step dancing through the figures.

I stick with the basic reels I have learned over the last couple of days, none of them as complicated as the ones I see here. I watch their feet intently and attempt to pick up steps here and there, trying them out in between sets. This is the way that step dancing has always been passed down from generation to generation, before there were dance masters who travelled from village to village teaching classes, before workshops and videos, when children would scrutinize their parents' and grandparents' feet on the dance floor and practice the steps until they came naturally.

Some say that Cape Breton step dancing is actually from Ireland, but they are in the minority. "When thousands upon thousands of Scottish Gaels were pouring into Cape Breton as immigrants," I'm told, "in amongst them, in an area very poor with no communications, no roads or anything, were about 500 people of Irish descent. It's hard to suppose that 500 Irishmen taught thousands of Highland Scots how to step dance. But that has been a controversy." It is most widely believed that step dancing was brought over to Cape Breton Island with immigrant settlers from the Outer Hebrides of Scotland, as well as some of the Inner Hebrides of the Gaelic speaking northwest coastal areas in the late 1700s and early 1800s.

At this time the Gaels were being evicted from their own country in favour of using the land for more profitable agricultural production. Searching for a place to re-settle, they landed in North America, in the maritime provinces of Canada, and especially in Nova Scotia. Although Pictou was the harbour town where most Gaels arrived, it would be the eastern counties of Nova Scotia and, in particular, Cape Breton that would preserve the Gaelic music and dance more than anywhere else in the world.

When the Gaels settled in Nova Scotia, step dancing was still a purely communal activity, not performed on a stage like it is today. As with Scotch music and storytelling, dance is a cultural manifestation of who the Gaels are, brought out during *ceilidhs* (gatherings) and parties. To have such a socially-based culture uproot and settle down in a new country brings with it an intact cultural structure, one that is still alive in Cape Breton.

What was sustained in Cape Breton by this mass immigration was an intensely Gaelic place where families and kinships could continue on as they might have in Scotland (if it weren't for the clearances, the First World War, and battles, of course). The isolation of the island – before a causeway was built in 1955, Cape Breton was accessible only by sea or air from the mainland of Nova Scotia – kept the new communities intact for the most part. In fact, I'm told there are quite a few grandparents in Cape Breton today, especially grandmothers, who do not even speak English.

Growing up in Gaelic Scotland or Nova Scotia meant being steeped in Scotch music from the womb, Gaelic storytelling before you could speak and dancing even as you learned to walk. Those were the living breaths of the Gaels and Cape Breton has kept that breathing alive today.

Much has also been lost. As with most orally-based cultures, the Gaels in Nova Scotia were soon put into schools where they were forced to learn English. Gaelic was forbidden and the stories that were hundreds of years old that they brought with them were considered useless. Instead, they were told to read books and study history on paper, which left many oral stories untold to the next generation.

I learn quickly, though, that the Gaelic spirit is still thriving at the Highland Village Museum in Iona. Jim Watson, the Gaelic Coordinator there, takes me through the 11 historic buildings that represent the domestic architecture of what would have been found in Gaelic Scotland around 1800 and Gaelic Nova Scotia from 1800 to the 1920s.

We go to the schoolroom where the Gaels were taught English and were banned from speaking their own language. Jim smiles slyly and says to me, "I'll tell you what we do here now. We push the desks back and we sing Gaelic songs, we dance and we play fiddle music!"

It's this compulsion to express themselves through song and dance that keeps the traditions alive. If a group has gathered and no one has a violin, for instance, someone will "jig a tune" (*port à beul*, or to make a tune from the mouth) so that the music can still be enjoyed and the dancers can still dance.

Songs stay alive in an old tradition called a "milling frolic," where the Gaelic speakers of the island gather. Even as they dwindle, especially in the older population, there is a whole new influx of people who want to learn Gaelic, and a milling frolic is a good place to start.

The next night I drive across the little bridge from the Highland Heights Inn, where I am staying beside the Village Museum, to Christmas Island. This isn't actually an island, but a tiny community with only a post office (where thousands send their letters at Christmastime to get them postmarked) and a firehall, where all the neighbourhood meetings and events take place.

I show up at the annual Gaelic festival, Féis an Eilein (Festival of the Island) to take part in the milling frolic. Because of the name, I imagine we will be nimbly dancing around a bonfire in the deepest recesses of a forest, fairylike and unshackled, but as soon as I step inside the small hall, I find out how completely wrong I am: a milling frolic is a group of people sitting around a wooden table singing Gaelic songs. They are not fairylike and they are not nimbly dancing. They are, however, having just as good a time.

Milling in Cape Breton, although it was done all over the world, comes from Scotland, where it is called waulking. Women would sew the ends of newly woven cloth together to make one circular piece and then dampen it with soap and water. Using a long table or even unhinging a door to work on, they pounded out the wet cloth on the table in order to shrink and soften it for warm clothing and blankets, singing songs in order to keep a steady rhythm and make the work more enjoyable. The last time waulking was done for utilitarian purposes is thought to be in the 1950s. Today, cloth doesn't need to be pounded by hand but the tradition is continued as a way to keep the songs alive.

In Scotland, this work was done by women, but here everyone joins in. In fact, it seems that men have overtaken women at the tables in Cape Breton, making up the majority of the singers. Their rich, deep tones mix with the one or two female voices at the table. Alternating between a soloist who starts a verse and the group who joins in for the chorus, each song is chosen by those at the table and often there is discussion about what will be sung next. In a modern touch tonight, there are microphones hanging on long poles from the ceiling that amplify the songs, delivering a remarkable chorus of Gaelic voices throughout the hall.

Speaking with Jim earlier in the day, he stressed the importance of song: "If you ask a Cape Bretoner of Gaelic-speaking background what they remember most about their grandparents, they will often say, 'there was always someone singing.'" Here it is evident that this is still true.

After hearing a few songs, I decide to take part, shyly taking a seat when a young man leaves. I don't speak a word of Gaelic and I can't carry a tune, so it's possible I might ruin this whole happy gathering. No matter, I am already sitting down and the gentleman across from me is asking the others what song they want to sing.

As his voice begins the first verse, those sitting at the table start pounding the white cloth in front of them. When it comes time for the chorus, everyone joins in by singing Gaelic words and vocables, equivalent to "la la la la la" or other sounds used to fill in the melody. I do my part by keeping the rhythm with the cloth and mimicking the mouth movements of the man across from me. The song is quite repetitive, so even though I can't understand what is being sung, I can at least hum along with the tune.

When the first song ends, I look around to see if anyone wants to kick me out. Instead, they are all smiling and someone comes by to sprinkle the cloth with some water, a symbolic gesture to remind us where this tradition comes from. So I stay, this time determined to join in on the vocals. As the next song begins, I again focus on the mouth of the man across the table from me. Pounding the cloth in rhythm, I begin to pick up the repeated words and recurring phrases; somehow I am able to stay afloat and, by the third song, I am starting to feel comfortable at my place at the table.

There is a break midway through the milling frolic to have tea and lunch. It's about 9:00 pm, an odd time for a lunch break, but here lunch retains its older meaning, that of a light meal or meal in between a more substantial dinner (which is what I would call lunch) and supper (which is what I would call dinner). We all gather in the tiny kitchen area of the firehall to drink tea and coffee, eat baked goods and bite-sized sandwiches, and to socialize with one another. Tonight again, I feel taken back in time.

Jim has been explaining to me what a *ceilidh* (pronounced kay-lee) is, a word I see on signs all throughout Nova Scotia and spoken by locals daily. I assume it's some kind of a party, because there's usually a meal and music involved, but I'm not entirely correct. The word translates to "a visit," or a gathering, although it is known by non-Gaelic speakers and tourists more as a performance with a fiddler and a dancer, often in a hall or an establishment that serves food. But a *ceilidh* is simply a get together where people tell stories, sing, dance, play tunes and connect with one another, sometimes in a hall but oftentimes in a house, a kitchen or a yard. They are never the same and have no format.

I get my first taste of one at the next day's afternoon *ceilidh* back at the Village Museum. Once a small group has gathered in the cozy living room of one of the old houses, this one a small family dwelling from 1829, Jim starts by telling some stories and answering questions from tourists who are eager to pick his knowledgeable mind about Gaelic history.

Laced in and out of the conversations, well-known Gaelic-speaking fiddler Joe Peter MacLean from nearby Boisdale, and Jim's son Colin play sporadic tunes on their violins, eliciting claps and much toe tapping. Joanne, a woman who works at the Village Museum, gets up periodically to step dance in a re-created folk costume.

Jim, Colin, Joe and Joanne speak in snippets to each other in Gaelic, switching to English to explain to us what they're saying; visitors are eager to share stories about their Scottish grandparents and their connection to Cape Breton. Most are here because of family ancestry and a curiosity to learn more about where they came from.

After the *ceilidh*, I ask Joanne about step dancing and am happy to get caught up in the middle of a conversation between her and Jim.

"I don't know how long I've been step dancing," starts Joanne. "It's one of those things you just kind of pick up around. At least, that's the way it used to be. I don't call myself a step dancer. Growin' up, everybody had enough to get through a set and if you had any interest, you tried to figure out some more steps. I mean, I've got like half a dozen steps – strathspey, half a dozen reel – but if somebody was to dance on stage, they aren't going to call me, they would get somebody with at least a dozen of each of those."

"Yeah, but I don't think we're talking about performance," interjects Jim. "We're talking about what the people know in the houses."

"Well, that's my point. I'm not a 'performer.'"

"And that's an important point, too," stresses Jim, "because Gaelic culture, singing and so forth… *a capella* singing was always the rule; nobody ever sang with musical accompaniment. That is all for commercial CD production, stage presentations and so forth. This is an utterly socially-based culture, the dancing is not performance, step dancing is not performed; people did this because they enjoyed it and it's just part of what you did. Utterly communal… people were not preparing for careers, this was just their cultural manifestation."

The evolution of Scotch music is similar. Are people playing too fast nowadays? Do they ornament the tunes or play the way it used to be played? Is there still Gaelic in fiddle music? The older generation is questioning what the younger generation is playing, who is pushing the boundaries of tradition. The issues are discussed often around the island and keep the culture alive, organic, and important.

Now there are classes offered in all of the Gaelic disciplines. With the development of step dancing classes and workshops for tourists, there still isn't an emphasis on competition, like Highland dancing, although there are step dancing competitions held outside of Cape Breton.

Jim continues: "That's a living community. When people are engaged and embrace that in large numbers, that's cultural transmission."

As much as Gaelic culture is interwoven into the fabric of Cape Breton, its potency has been diluted over the years. Fewer locals have been showing up at the summer dances and the older Gaelic speakers are passing away (although a new, younger generation of people interested in learning Gaelic is on the rise, a hopeful trend).

On my two visits to Cape Breton, even though the rhythm of the Gaels was something I came across everyday, steeped in the ground I walked on, most locals said that the culture is less dominant than it once was.

Jim tells me, "Even when you look at dance and music in Cape Breton today, compared to what it was 25 or 30 years ago, it's only a small bit of what's left."

***

Back at the dance at Glencoe Mills, all of this newfound information hadn't popped my fairytale experience, but my conversations over the last few days did make me aware of the precarious state of the culture. The good news? Glencoe was packed with people of all ages that evening, dancing the sets they had known since they were children and step dancing to the tunes they grew up hearing. It was just as full when the dance ended early the next morning.

I left Glencoe feeling optimistic that the Gaelic ways would be remembered and carried on by the passionate younger generation, people who are finding their way through the old traditions and adding their contemporary stamp.

There's a wonderful documentary that was made by Genuine Pictures Inc. for Bravo! called, *And They Danced*. Filmed all over Cape Breton, my dancing partner Burton is one of the main characters featured throughout and, when asked about Glencoe, he laughs: "Quite often when you go to a dance at Glencoe, you will be driving along and all of a sudden you'll see someone in front of you…So you'll stop and say, 'Are you lost?' 'Yes, we're trying to find Glencoe.' 'Well, follow me,' [I say]. How do you get to Glencoe? You go until you're lost and then you're there." Which is exactly the right way to learn how to step dance.

It is half way through my trip when it comes time to celebrate my August birthday. I sleep in at the Highland Heights Inn and make my way downstairs for a cup of tea overlooking the Bras d'Or Lake. A scattering of wooden tables are set up in the hotel restaurant with large windows presenting the lake below like a living painting.

I smile as I remember fiddler Joe MacLean playing during an impromptu *ceilidh* here the other day at lunch. We all sat quietly enjoying the warm summer day when Joe turned from his food and picked up his violin. The room was filled with tune after tune, everyone tapping their feet in rhythm. A young Irishwoman whom I would meet later at a square dance got up and did some Irish step dancing in between tables, delighted at the opportunity to dance during lunch. I can't remember what I ate, but it was the best meal of the trip.

As these memories swim through my head, I finish off my tea and get my things together for a full day out and about the island. I'm heading west to Judique to see the exhibits on Cape Breton dancing and have lunch at the Celtic Music Interpretive Centre. Once there, I sit down at my table and get ready to enjoy the lunch *ceilidh* and notice a familiar head in front of me – it's Burton! "Oh, I'm at everything," he jokes.

We settle in for lunch at the centre's small eatery and I look up on the stage to see Brandi, whom I had met at Glencoe the other night, and who will be both playing some tunes on the fiddle and step dancing. Burton, the dance enthusiast that he is, ends up joining her on stage to show off a few of his signature moves.

After I finish my pan fried haddock, mashed potatoes, coleslaw and blueberry pie lunch, Brandi comes over and says to me, "Hey, we met at Glencoe, right?" I tell her that we did and that it's a surprise to see her again. "Oh, we all get around," she laughs. "It's a small island."

This is the beauty of a place like Cape Breton: you can travel here as a first time tourist and leave knowing half of the island, as was evident when I told Burton where I was going that night. Up in Chéticamp, over 100 km north on highway 19 and just at the foot of the Cape Breton Highlands National Park and the Cabot Trail, I had a ticket to an Acadian step dancing performance going on in one of the schools. Burton has been meaning to check it out and he knows the Artistic Director, Paul Gallant, from way back, so we decide the best thing to do is to go together.

I want to stay at the Celtic Centre for another hour or so, so I plan to meet Burton later in the afternoon at his place in Whycocomagh. I go through the small exhibit set up by the centre that features the music, dancing and key people behind the survival of these traditions in Cape Breton. Most exciting for me is the interactive step dancing section where I can follow along with a video and learn the basics of stepping on a re-created porch. There are also fiddles to play, which I try, but it doesn't go so well, so I stick to dancing. I might have even scared a few people away from the exhibit space with my screechy playing.

Brandi comes in while I'm practicing some reels with the video and offers to teach me more complicated steps. We run through about four different reels and three different strathspeys, each a bit more difficult than the last. A trick that she uses for students who haven't grown up listening to fiddle tunes and watching step dancers' feet, is to make simple rhythms in your head: for jigs, which are done during square sets, she tells me to repeat "Jig-gid-y, jig-gid-y," accounting for all three beats on each foot. For reels, faster and more complicated, she uses the phrase, "This-is-how-a-reel-goes" to beat out all six steps. For strathspeys, four beats can be remembered with "Co-ca-co-la."

Within each of the reels and strathspeys, there are many more to learn, and new ones are being created all the time. Dancers will watch one another at dances all over the island to see what kind of steps they have come up with and often teach them to each other, spreading them around the communities.

As well as tapping out the right beats to the right part of the tune (a reel is stepped when a reel is played on the fiddle or bagpipes, for example), there is a very specific style of movement that all step dancers in Cape Breton follow and is different from that done anywhere else in the world.

Here, movement happens almost solely from the knees down. The upper body and arms stay relaxed and, although they bounce with the steps, are kept still in order to keep the focus on their footwork. This footwork is low to the ground and doesn't move around, always staying light. In the past, good step dancers would dance on just the circumference of tree stumps that were only 16 inches square and could still dance even if they were crammed in a tiny space during a kitchen party. There was no "audience," so the steps were kept nearly imperceptible underneath themselves and didn't include kicking their legs up, for example, like Irish step dancing.

They strived to dance *with* the fiddler, this musical bond being the most important connection for dancer and musician as they supported each other throughout each tune. Because the two are intrinsically entwined, they have now been better preserved than if they had been entirely separate disciplines.

Just before leaving the Celtic centre for the afternoon, I buy my first Scotch CD, Donald Angus Beaton's *Live at the house*. It was recommended to me by Jim who told me, "It's just some recordings they made of him in the house. He's from the coal mines down there, playing these old tunes, you know. That's Scotch music. That's Gaelic music. Just terrific."

With Donald Angus Beaton tunes filling my rental car, I follow the directions I was given to Burton's house in Whycocomagh. There is more country road driving and somehow I end up passing a parish hall that seems oddly familiar: is that Glencoe? It looks much different (and easier to find) in the daylight. I inevitably get lost on a deserted dirt road, not even sure which direction I'm heading in. I finally see a couple driving towards me and I slow down, hoping they can help. They stop their car beside mine and smile, knowing that I'm lost. The confusion on my face must be obvious.

The man driving gives me simple instructions to get me back onto the main road, where I'll see the signs for Whycocomagh. The town is mostly built along the main street, so it's unmistakable once you hit the paved road. Just as Burton and the couple had described, I hit the main street, drive into town, and find the house right away. Burton comes out as I'm parking the car in his driveway and invites me inside to meet his family.

His brother is home, so we are introduced and I'm welcomed to Cape Breton. The small house is simply decorated with old fashioned furniture and littered with family photos in vintage frames. Before I can spend much more time looking around, Burton bounces in with a birthday gift he put together this afternoon: a Cape Breton Fiddler's Association cookbook (which I still have) and a small Cape Breton flag (which I have sitting in a thriving aloe vera plant in my living room). He will also treat me to dinner in a small seafood diner in Chéticamp before the show.

Much more fiddle music is played in Burton's car on the way to Chéticamp, although Burton assures me that the people here do listen to music *other* than the fiddle. Chéticamp is the largest centre of the Acadian population in Cape Breton – descendants of the French colonists who settled here in the 17th century – where you're greeted with "Bonjour" before "Hello." I had heard about Acadian step dancing but wasn't sure exactly how it differed from the more well known Cape Breton step dancing.

We arrive at the school early ("We are located next to the big church in the NDA School [French language school]… you cannot miss it; there's only one street in Chéticamp," wrote Paul, the Artistic Director of the show, in an earlier email) to meet the dancers and have them break down for me what we will see during the performance.

As soon as we walk into the backstage area at school, Burton and Paul (who doesn't know that I'm bringing anyone) greet each other enthusiastically and do some catching up. There is also a mother there who is getting her daughter ready and she remembers Burton from years ago. We all chat about Acadian step dancing and the teenaged dancers show me some of the steps that they've been practicing and tell me about how much they love performing with each other.

The group, called La Swing du Suête, is a collection of adorable children and includes an especially talented seven-year-old girl, a younger sister of one of the dancers, who has an astonishing knack for step dancing at lighting quick speed, without missing a beat. She effortlessly steals the show.

The first thing I notice about Acadian-style step dancing is the speed at which the fiddlers play. The tempo is upped a notch from what I had been hearing so far, the dancers telling me beforehand that the fiddlers speed up so much because they get so excited by the music and end up playing as fast as they can. "So we have to dance faster, too," they giggle.

There certainly isn't the obvious low-to-the-ground emphasis on footwork like the Cape Breton style, but there aren't any flashy kicks either (like Michael Flatley in the Irish Riverdance). Their footwork also has a stomping element to it, more like clogging.

The show itself is highly energetic and the children put everything they have into the performance. At the end of the show I find myself thinking how I'm just a half an hour's drive away from the heart of Gaelic Nova Scotia, which is a completely different world than this.

***

My last day in Cape Breton is inevitable. I spend it on the beach writing, relaxing and remembering everyone I have met here. The finale of my trip is also the culmination of the *féis* and they do it in style by throwing a family square dance (what else would be expected?) at the Christmas Island firehall.

I eat my last halibut supper at the Highland Heights Inn and make the three minute drive from Iona to Christmas Island for the 9:00 pm start. Although square dancing happens every night during the summer months at different community halls in Inverness County (and across the island), the sets are different depending on which area you are in. Sometimes there are two sets of jigs and a reel played, sometimes the traditional grouping of four couples in a square is expanded to fit in more pairs; it all depends on the region. West Mabou is not the same as Christmas Island; Southwest Margaree is not the same as Glencoe. So wherever you go to a dance in Cape Breton, the formations are different and the amount of step dancing you see within the figures will vary.

It certainly keeps me on my toes, but it's easy to get the hang of things. As Brandi told me at the Celtic Music Centre, "It's been the same [square] dance set for the last forever many years." Once you know it, you know it for life. What started as four-hand and eight-hand Reels from Scotland has adapted over the years depending on the community they are danced in and the people who dance them, but if I come back in 10 years, I could probably still fit in with the sets that I learned on this trip.

What I have been hearing from the locals, unfortunately, is that less Cape Bretoners are going to the dances, but more tourists are attending, which is great, except that it means the majority of people don't actually know what they're doing once they get up on the dance floor. I found this at some of the dances, yet at others, like Glencoe, this wasn't the case at all, with people gently pushing me in the right direction if I was heading the wrong way. The island has known this kind of flux before, and has gotten through what could have been a crisis.

It happened in the early 1970s when the CBC made a documentary called *The Vanishing Cape Breton Fiddler*, telling the story of the violin in Cape Breton from introduction to the decline of players at that time. When the film came out, it was a shock to some that what was once the lifeline for Nova Scotian culture was disappearing, while others were outraged that such a statement could even be made: fiddling was going strong but being kept alive in a quieter way. This lead to a resurgence in fiddling that continues to this day. Since the summer I was in Cape Breton, I have heard there are more locals attending dances again.

I remember a boy from Boston (where there is also a huge Gaelic population) at the *féis* named Ross, who couldn't have been more than 11 years old. We immediately connected because he was wearing a Pittsburgh Penguins t-shirt the first time I saw him and I'm a huge Pens fan.

I would see him during the festival lending a hand whenever he was needed and jumping in to participate wherever he could. We sat at the same milling frolic table and we even took a semi-private step dancing lesson together. We got to chatting and he told me that he had come up with his family, as they do every year, to help out at the *féis*. That has got to be a positive sign for the years to come.

***

Only one island over and separated by the Cabot Strait is Newfoundland, where traditional dance is not as much a part of the contemporary folk scene as it is in Cape Breton, and is a challenge for travellers to find. The province of Newfoundland and Labrador certainly has its dancers, and enthusiastic they are, but these days there seems to be less communities where dancing is a part of people's everyday lives. For the most part, it's done on special occasions or when someone makes the effort to arrange an event.

"Dance, sadly, is one of the – not one of – it *is* the weakest folk tradition in the province," Jane Rutherford tells me over a cup of tea in Vancouver. As well as her "day job" with the Government of Canada, Jane has a "hobby job" as a traditional dancer. She has travelled widely in Newfoundland and Labrador and collects traditional dances in communities where people are still dancing or have memories of dances. In a couple of communities with dances on the brink of being lost, she has worked with community members to revive a dance by doing interviews with seniors who, decades ago, were dancers or dance musicians. Piecing together their memories and using her knowledge of similar set dances, she has been able to re-create a dance and then teach it to a group of adults or kids in the community. She loves showing the newly-revived dance to the seniors, as when they see it, more memories are sometimes sparked. They enjoy giving their feedback on what is correct and what needs tweaking.

On a similar project, Jane worked with accordion player Stan Pickett to re-create a dance from his home community of Fair Island in Bonavista Bay. The inhabitants of Fair Island were resettled by 1961 as part of a government program to encourage the abandonment of communities with "no great future." With the community gone and the population dispersed, as well as the gaining popularity of nightclubs – Saturday night dances were filled with country music provided by bands in the mainland communities where those from the islands settled – it's no wonder the people of Fair Island had nearly forgotten a dance that was hugely popular in the 1950s. Stan and Jane viewed segments of the dance preserved on videos and Stan had lots of memories playing for dances when he was a teenager. Between them they re-created the Fair Island Square Dance and presented it as a paper and workshop at the 2008 North Atlantic Fiddle Convention held in St. John's that year.

"They traditionally had benches on the dance floor – they did the dance with 16 people in one set – so when the ends were dancing, the sides sat on the bench and then the reverse. The hall where they used to have the dances was one of these special places for men that occasionally women and children were allowed into when they had these big community events," Jane says, sharing some of the memories that Stan passed along on the dances in Fair Island.

"[Stan] said they would often have two sets on the floor at a time, the hall filled to capacity and the benches lined up, with him in the middle playing the button accordion. When we performed the dance at this international conference, we didn't have benches, so we used chairs. People were really amused to see these chairs on the dance floor. And we practiced, because Stan was explaining how (he has so many memories of the dance growing up) the dancers were to get from the chair into the dance, how it had to be a smooth move.

"You joined your arms together and you had to flow up from the chair. We practiced that a lot! Right on the music. And at the end of your turn (ends or sides of the set), at the exact moment you put your bum on the chair is at the exact point in the music – it [became] part of the dance."

The dances that arrived in Newfoundland came from Europe and have left their mark in the set dances used today, dances like the lancers from England or the cotillion from France. Jane tells me that different communities have their unique versions of a dance – the lancers as danced in the community of Branch today is quite different to how they do it Burin, for example, and a set dancer from Ireland might not even recognize either of these dances as the lancers.

The set dances were learned in a similar way as in Cape Breton. "Calling would be from inside the set," says Jane, "just muttering to each other what's coming up next. So the dances were never traditionally taught, they were learned by osmosis, kids hanging around the edge of the hall, being pushed around when they were big enough to get into the set. That's the way the dances were traditionally. Nowadays, groups that are still dancing are keen to learn other dances. People get together to 'swap' their dances and sometimes I've been asked to teach a group a dance from another part of the province."

Jane is one of the staff members at Vinland Music Camp, an all ages folk camp that takes place every year in Gros Morne National Park in western Newfoundland. Traditional dancing is one of the courses at the week-long camp and every night there is a camp dance with a great dance band.

"It's really fun to have the range of ages at the camp," says Jane, "as we're all there for the same reason – a love of traditional music and dance. Differences between the generations fade into the background for the week, except when it comes to picking up new tunes or dances. The youngsters always seem to be able to learn new pieces so quickly, leaving the adults feeling like their memory skills have seen better days. Thankfully," she laughs, "the kids don't seem to mind too much waiting for their older classmates to catch up.

"One of the things I love about leading dances is seeing how much fun people have. Some might hesitate at first about joining in but there's safety in numbers – you're part of a group and I demonstrate the footwork and say, 'Anyone can do this. Here's the footwork in Newfoundland set dancing.' [She demonstrates simply stepping one foot in front of the other and laughs.] I really make the point that it's a dance you do for fun...

"We do school tours as well with Vinland Music. I've had some really big sessions. In one community on the Northern Peninsula, one of my colleagues had six or eight kids in his guitar workshop and I had about 100 in the school gym for the dance workshop. This massive army of dancers! With that number of people you can't do a regular set dance, so I adapt things to the numbers. Newfoundland set dances tend to be quite long and quite complex, traditionally the dances are done – not all communities are dancing communities – but those that are often only have one or two dances that they would do and they would do it all night. One dance could take 20 minutes or even longer."

One of the most beautiful set dances in Newfoundland, in Jane's view, is "Running the Goat," a dance known more in St. John's than rurally and which a section of was performed at the Winter Olympics in Vancouver. It was collected in the early 1980s by a group called Sheila's Brush, a music, dance and folklore troupe. The dance is from Harbour Deep, another community that was resettled and no longer exists. Sheila's Brush videoed the dance, adapted it and added some showy bits. There is a great figure called "Cracking the Whip" that isn't traditional but is almost always used today because it's fun and flashy. The group travelled around performing the Goat and people loved the fast speed of the dance, the way the shape of the set changed from "longways" to a square to a circle, staying fluid while being dynamic.

Even though these dances come mostly from Europe, Newfoundlanders tend to identify specifically with their Irish roots. As Kristin Harris Walsh writes in her paper "How Irish is Irish: Identity in Irish-Newfoundland Step Dancing," a majority of the province's population is actually of English descent: "Newfoundlanders as a people have tended to naturalize an Irish identity that binds them together, regardless of individuals' personal ancestry." Irish-Newfoundland stepping came over with the Christian Brothers in 1876 as they taught Catholic in the school system and only became part of the school curriculum in St. John's as late as the 1930s.

"The ideological links between Ireland and Newfoundland," writes Kristin earlier in her paper, "are rooted in a myriad of commonalities, some tangible, others intangible, all highly symbolic. From landscape to ethnic stereotype, Ireland and Newfoundland share perceived and real similarities that have enabled and perhaps encouraged Newfoundland culture to model itself after that of Ireland. Nowhere is this more prevalent than in the arts."

For visitors who want a taste of this, though, it is difficult to find people doing traditional dancing on a regular basis here. Large dances might pop up sporadically, but the best time to see dancing is in the summer during the Newfoundland and Labrador Folk Festival, where you'll likely see the Goat in some shape or form. There's also Sound Traditions in Salmonier, a three-day music and dance retreat for adults in the fall, and over on the west coast of the island is the week-long Vinland Music Camp, where music and dance workshops have been going on since 2001.

Otherwise, Dale Jarvis is doing his part as the Intangible Cultural Heritage Development Officer employed by the provincial government. He is involved with events all over the province that foster intangible heritage in Newfoundland and Labrador, safeguarding and sustaining this knowledge for future generations. He quite possibly has the best job title in the world.

***

Back in Cape Breton, I can only believe that the people here will never stop dancing. So far they have protected their heritage, making this a very special place to live and visit, and that wouldn't be the same without the fiddle and summer dances.

***

I had never heard of phosphorescent water before but after my last square dance in Christmas Island, I followed the crowd down to a hidden beach not far away. Here, we all gathered to extend the festivities and I sat down on some rocks beside the Barra Strait. It was completely dark except for a few car lights and the air was filled with laughter and high spirits.

I was sitting with one of the dancers and he casually started to throw sand into the phosphorescent water. To my astonishment, each grain sparkled like fairy dust, creating a shimmering dance against the otherwise pitch black sky.

CANADA

New Brunswick

Fredericton

USA

3 New Brunswick: Flinging through the Highland Games

On the verge of waking up, I hear the sound of bagpipes in the distance. Confused, I turn onto my left side and force my eyes open: I notice I'm in a hotel room, in the standard North American style, so why does it sound like Scotland?

Groggily dragging my body to the window, I pull back the curtains to see a healthy amount of fog sitting cosily over the water, the sun barely trying to break through. It looks like Scotland, it sounds like Scotland, but I am actually staying at the Delta hotel in downtown Fredericton.

It is the first morning of the New Brunswick Highland Games and the pipers are already out on the fields practising for the weekend competition, their pipes overriding each other in a discord of melodies. These sounds will become my soundtrack over the next few days.

Jasmin Astle is 17 years old when I meet her at the games, a local Highland dancer and piper who also step dances and has played the fiddle. Her Scottish roots are from her father's side, as her great grandmother was originally from Scotland and her great grandfather was from a small community on the Gaspé Peninsula in Quebec that's nicknamed "wee Scotland" because of its history as a Scottish settlement.

She agrees to help educate me in being Scottish this weekend by teaching me some Highland dance and giving me pointers so I can watch the dance competition with an expert eye, or at least a semi-knowledgeable one. Unfortunately, watching a Highland dance competition is not the most entertaining activity one can engage in.

Each competitor is judged on his or her solo performance, but dances on stage in a small group with others his or her own age (mostly her). For sometimes an hour at a time, the same tune plays for each group and the same steps are danced, giving the judges a chance to see every dancer do every step. I learn pretty quickly that it's fantastic in small doses but frequent breaks for the spectator are essential.

It wasn't always so. Not until an early Highland Society *ceòl mór* (classic) piping competition in Edinburgh around 1783 did Highland dancing appear in the program at the games at all. It proved very popular and by 1785, it had been promoted from post-competition to within the competition, performed in between the regular piping program. Dancers were almost exclusively competing pipers who could also dance, meaning they were all men. The only woman recorded as taking part was in 1799 when she was brought in for entertainment, according to the densely researched book, *Traditional Gaelic Bagpiping* by John G. Gibson.

The first formally organized Highland games happened in Strathfillan, Scotland in 1819. From then on, Highland dancing would evolve, using classical ballet feet and arm positions as a base, and change drastically from a men's only activity to an almost exclusively female one in Canada today.

Halifax saw the first organized games in 1860, with Antigonish in 1863 and New Glasgow following shortly afterwards. The Caledonian Club of Prince Edward Island, a group formed to promote awareness of and take pride in their Scottish heritage, first met around this time and had their first Highland games in Charlottetown in 1864. The New Brunswick Highland Games are much younger, having opened in 1982.

The games were originally created in response to the Northern Meeting, a social event that was organized in Inverness in 1798. A party of balls, live music, dining and horse races, the event was really an English-speaking affair for gentry, which offended the Gaels. They in turn formed an organization called Commun nam Fìor Ghàidheal (Society of the True Gaels), which was among the ones that began formalizing piping into a competition for Highland games.

Before any of the formal competitions started, though, dancing happened between friends and communities in homes and at the pub. Men would play a game called "Smàladh na Coinnle" (smearing or snuffing the candle). It was either played by men having to flick the top of a burning wick with their foot without putting out the flame, or extinguishing the flame between the heels of their shoes, all while continuing to dance.

Eventually there would only be two men left and they would have to "dance it out" on blocks of wood, small slabs elevated up off the ground and spanning little more than 30 centimetres (12 inches) around. Whoever could do the most complete steps was declared the winner.

Out on the land, Highland dancing was a male celebration and test of strength and agility. It is said that old kings and chiefs would choose the best men out of the dancers to fill their ranks, as these would invariably be the most athletic and have the best stamina as warriors.

This love of dancing as it permeated through Scottish culture led to more and more of it being included in the games, albeit in a more refined manner. None of the standards of judging are known, nor was any of the music written down, so it's hard to be sure which songs were used and how the dancers were adjudicated.

By 1817, dance had become an audience favourite. In an effort to improve the games and increase interest from the public, a wider range of dances were included, as well as cash incentives offered; eventually there were prizes for best dressed and best homemade tartans. No longer were they only competing pipers, but dancers in their own right.

The Gaels have been dancing since we have written records but to do so in a formal competition was something altogether new. This 19th century change of format from casual *ceilidhs*, weddings and post-marching days for the army, would completely alter the state of Scottish dancing. As John G. Gibson so succinctly writes in his book, the games were just staged events to put "Highlandism" into a modern British framework to the denigration of older Gaelic traditions.

The spontaneity of both piping and dancing would make way for organized competitions and performances, and piping would lose some of its traditional sound as it became used for the more refined contemporary Highland dancing; the Gaels' love of physical challenges was also formalized in the 19th century, as events like caber tossing and hammer throwing were created, events that are still used in competition today.

Although done with the aim of "improvement," this progress also changed the traditions greatly. Contemporary Highland games that we see all over the world now probably don't resemble what the Gaels were doing a couple of hundred years ago as much as people may think.

As the number of dances increased over those early years, now this repertoire has dwindled to a measly handful that are used at Highland games today. The Mac an Fhorsair, for example, had died out by 1822. Although there were reports that it might have been danced in Nova Scotia, it is completely gone now. This limited number of dances made it easier for judges to give scores, as they only had to know certain steps, and teachers only taught their students what was required for competition. Young dancers today are learning just a fraction of the dances that their ancestors knew and, as the older generation passes away, they take the seldom-practiced dances with them to the grave.

Whether this is disastrous or just a part of evolution, or both, is up for debate. Although some purists wish the dances could be preserved more strictly, many in the Highland community enjoy how the art form is changing. As long as the tradition keeps developing, and it is based on what has come before, then dances will live on in each future generation.

At the New Brunswick Highland Games, a competition called the East Coast Choreography Challenge was created in this spirit. Using only the criteria that the piece must have a Scottish theme, music or costume, the choreographers are allowed to fuse in any type of movement they want. This allows both the dancers and teachers to stray from the defined rules that now govern Highland dancing.

There were two groups competing during the year I attended. The first were three girls from 13 to 15 years old from Fredericton who had been given a key to the dance studio and the freedom to choreograph the routine and design the costumes for themselves.

Dressed in maids' attire with tartan vests and using brooms as props, they fused a story about three unhappy maids who shed their aprons and brooms to bask in their newfound freedom. Although Highland steps are used throughout, the girls sprinkled in a few fun kicks and Broadway-type moves with their hats, while following the beats of a song that could have been used as the soundtrack for a Sherlock Holmes movie.

Their competition was another group of three girls, these from the College of Piping and Celtic Performing Arts of Canada in nearby Prince Edward Island, and who looked about 16 or 17 years old. Wearing soft, deep red dresses cut halter top style with flowing, knee-length skirts and red, black and white tartan sashes, the girls twirled and soared with Highland steps and epic bagpipe music. Theirs was a more polished Scottish number and ended up winning the hearts of the judges, who gave them first prize.

What this leaves us with is a strong base of dancers who have been trained traditionally, albeit learning a limited number of dances, and who are eager to compete by the rules set out by the contemporary Highland dance board. But these same students are also adding other genres of steps into creations of their own, mixing movements popular from the past with those popular now.

The rest of the Fredericton competition is standard and repetitive. The Highland Fling, the Reel, the Sailor's Hornpipe, the Sword Dance, the Seann Triubhas and the Irish Jig dances are repeated by small groups of competitors, each having its own story and history to be performed in corresponding costumes. Age determines which dances each girl or boy must perform, making it easier for the judges to adjudicate.

Even though I'm an adult, I must go back to the basics if I want to learn Highland dance properly. Jasmin gathers me and a group of six people and leads us into a yellow and white striped tent set up for dance workshops. There are two wobbly pieces of plywood set down on the grass, acting as a stage, a plastic table covered in sample costumes that Jasmin has brought in, and fold up chairs set out in eight rows for those who don't want to dance themselves but are interested in learning about it.

"So, only two of you want to join me?" asks Jasmin playfully, after noticing that only one other young woman plus myself have stepped onto the plywood stage.

"Don't be scared, I'm starting you right from the beginning!" But no one moves in their seats except for the occasional squirm and self-conscious smile.

The first thing we're taught is called a *pas de basque*, which is a main step in the Sword Dance. It is also one of the first steps youngsters as little as two years old learn in their first Highland dance classes. I guess we are starting right from the beginning.

With pointed toes, we move back and forth from one foot to the other with two steps on the spot in between, the first step on the ball of the foot. It's almost like a waltz but instead of whirling around the room, we move from side to side with turned out legs.

"And now high cuts!" Jasmin shouts over the pre-recorded pipe music, which mingles with the live pipers warming up on the other side of the field. Here we switch to quick slicing movements, continuing to jump from one foot to the other but pointing the back foot up to the back of our other calf. We start alternating between *pas de basque* and high cuts, doing six *pas de basque* and four quick high cuts to complete a phrase of the music. After a few repetitions, Jasmin stops the music and we stand there panting like dogs that have been chasing their tails in the desert, our calves about to burst into flames.

"Now, we learn the arms," Jasmin continues, barely winded. You'll often see Highland dancers with their arms slightly rounded up in the air like a fifth position in ballet. Their fingers differ completely, though: instead of lengthened, evenly spaced fingers, they must place their thumbs in contact with the first joint of their middle fingers, their pointers sticking straight out; the next finger points a little bit higher than the middle fingers but below the pointers, and their pinkies stick straight up in the air like they're drinking English tea.

This position is said to replicate that of the stag, the upraised arms and fingers acting as antlers. It was the most common theory I was given by dancers for the reasoning behind the position, but historical books also point out that the hands could have been lifted for help with balance and the stag imitation added as a more modern stylization. Regardless, dancers nowadays hold fast to the stag interpretation and are required to use this placement in competition.

The *pas de basque* and high cuts make up part of the Sword Dance, or Gille Callum. Jasmin tells us that in competition, swords are laid down on the ground and you can't touch any part of them while dancing. It is the only Highland dance where you are allowed to look down at your feet while competing, but if you touch a sword, you are disqualified immediately.

I chat with Jasmin's mother this weekend, too, and she recounts that when her daughter was a child, she would watch her do the sword dance with concern. "It's the only dance where you're allowed to look at your feet –

but she didn't. The first few times she did it, I would hold my breath because I didn't know how she did that without tripping. And I nearly passed out from holding my breath! She'd be going around the swords and she wouldn't look down. And I was like, 'Honey, that's the one you can look down.' So we had to train her to look down for the Sword Dance."

If Jasmin had done this out on the war field in the distant past, not looking down could have been a fatal mistake. There are many theories about where this dance comes from, all of them containing real swords. Some say it was a pre-battle dance to bring good luck to the side of the dancer and bad luck to his opponents. The direction in which he danced around the swords was said to have been important, although modern accounts vary on which direction meant good luck and which meant bad luck. Either way, if he touched one of the swords while dancing, it meant doom for him in the impending battle, and if many of his fellow soldiers also touched theirs, it was a sure defeat for their side.

Others say this was a post-battle dance where soldiers would do a victory dance over the swords of their conquests. This theory dates back to the time of King Malcolm Canmore in the 11th century. There was a Highland dancer whom everyone knew named Ghillie Callum, acknowledged as the best in Scotland. He may have even been a Celtic prince. In the Battle of Dunsinane (or Battle of Dundee), it is said he killed MacBeth, crossed his sword over his slain opponent, and danced in his triumphant conquest.

Still some say that the dance involved the decapitated head of MacBeth, so dancers now have to decide for themselves how gory they want the back story to be. As one dance teacher told me of today's adaptation where dancers are disqualified for touching the fake swords, "It's not quite as gruesome, but it's definitely bad luck!"

This takes us to the Highland Fling, probably the most recognized and oldest of all Scottish dances, and potentially as bloody as the Sword Dance. After a battle victory, clansmen are said to have taken their *targe*, a small shield that had a spike of steel in the centre – some say five to six inches long – laid it on the ground and danced on top of it. With the spike sticking straight up, the warriors had to rely on their dexterity and quick footwork while dancing completely on the spot to avert injury. This celebratory dance is based on the movements of a stag, the fancy footwork like a deer prancing and the arms held in a fifth position above the head with antler-like fingers.

Today's dancers don't much resemble their historic counterparts and only have to move around the steel spike in their imaginations. They keep the spirit of the tradition alive by dancing in one spot and high on the balls of their feet, but the focus is more on ballet-inspired technique and positioning. Given the history of the dance, it's ironic that this is usually the first dance little children are taught, although I'm sure they aren't given all of the gory details.

Dancers must complete some of the eight steps in the Fling (depending on age and level) in a normal competition, but when they are competing for a championship, the Scottish Official Board chooses set steps that each dancer must do. Called "championship steps," they change order every year so the students don't know what to practise until the steps are decided on. Although there are a few ways of doing each step (regions and countries sometimes differ on the corner they point to, or other minor variations), they are written down step-by-step in a book.

The dance most closely resembling old Scotland is the Highland Reel, forms of it being danced in remote parts of the Highlands almost exclusively until 1875. There are various setting steps that are danced on the spot, alternating with a travelling figure that usually repeats throughout. The dance was never really about learning the steps as much as it was about enjoying the company of those in the room and being able to rejoice in the music that is one of the most binding aspects of Scottish culture.

At the turn of the century and as dance became more formalized, young men were taught specifically how to ask a girl to dance ("May I have the pleasure of this dance?"), as well as the proper behaviour to accompany the question. He would be taught to stand in front of her with his heels together and bow before asking her, and if she said "yes," he would offer her his arm and lead her to the dance floor. At night balls, they would bring a flower for their partner and it's said that if they were courting a particular girl, they would also buy her ball shoes.

Girls were taught to behave modestly and wore white dresses to the night balls with inch-high heels. The women who went to public dances were almost exclusively single, as it was somewhat improper to attend as a married woman, or man. This caused the dancers to generally be young and the music played catered to the modern dances being introduced from elsewhere, rather than traditional dances of the generation before.

There was also a switch in music tempo, as it picked up in speed. Where once only the upper classes danced, with women wearing immense, hooped skirts, fashions changed and so did the ability for women to be unencumbered by their elaborate dress. Tempos quickened and the lower classes joined in on the fun.

As the twentieth century progressed, World War I was greatly responsible for wiping out a lot of the old dances. The new ones from all over Europe like the quadrille, waltz and polka became favourites after the war was over and people wanted dances filled with high tempos and uplifting tunes. After World War II and the popularity of jazz and ballroom dances like the foxtrot, one step and quick step were established, traditional dances were forgotten.

The Reel itself was evolving, as dance masters taught classical ballet positions to refine the steps. They weren't called first, second, third, fourth and fifth positions at that time, but the ballet terms were eventually used, as they are today. Traditionally, dancers would form a circle and follow each other through the travelling steps. This became a dance for three or more people to do the setting steps on the spot and then move into a figure during the travelling steps.

This old dance became refined and standardized throughout the 1900s and is now performed at Highland games strictly with four dancers who travel in a figure eight during competition. The dancers are judged as soloists with well-defined criteria for their timing, technique and general deportment while on stage.

The most historically significant Highland dance is the Seann Triubhas. In and around 1790, a dance formed with movements like the dancers were shedding their trousers. They called it *seann triubhas*, which translates from Gaelic as "old trousers." It started off slowly as the trousers were shrugged off before the tune sped up and the movements turned into celebratory fling-like steps to rejoice in the freedom of wearing their kilts and tartans.

It was created in response to The Act of Proscription (1747) and the Disarming Act (1716), which were repealed in 1782. They had outlawed anyone who had a "warlike weapon." These acts were part of an effort to disarm the Highlanders and weaken their defence. The newer act went farther than the original by adding a section that forbade the wearing of "Highland Clothes" like "the plaid, philibeg, or little kilt, trowse, shoulder belts, or any part whatsoever of what peculiarly belongs to the highland garb." The penalty was six months in prison with no bail for a first offence and "transported to any of his Majesty's plantations beyond the seas, there to remain for a space of seven years" if committed again.

Disappointingly, I learn from Jasmin that the tartans the girls wear in today's competitions do not usually date back to that time or follow their family's lineage. The "kilts" are, in fact, pleated or kilted skirts (traditional kilts are worn by men) and the tartans are chosen, not for their clan affiliation, but because of price.

"Some of the tartans are much more expensive," Jasmin tells me plainly. "You have to order them specifically and have them woven if it's not a common one. So you often see lots of the same kilts with dancers because those are the ones you don't have to order specially... You just pick out the one you like. It doesn't have to be a family tartan. They always have to be a direct tartan, though, which means they have white in them... I think it's mainly because it looks better on stage. When you have a dark tartan, you can't see the colours so well, but with the white, it makes the colours stand out."

The way Highland dancing has survived today parallels how the world has changed. The Gaels were spontaneous, boisterous people who danced to express themselves and to one up their friends in neighbourhood pubs, but as the world around them became more industrialized and filled with new rules, Highland dancing become gradable and competitive. It is now performed at Highland games around the world and dancers compete in a circuit for medals and prize money.

Judges follow the Scottish Official Board of Highland Dancing's book and adjudicate dances on their ballet-like technique and poise; they must see that the dancer is hitting all the right positions while appearing completely at ease. The board was formed in 1950 for just this purpose. Organizations at the time were complaining that some of the judging was unfair and that dancers had to adjust their style and steps to correspond with the region they were competing in. Judges were adjudicating more from their own personal and regional preferences than from the actual technique being performed.

Standardization allows dancers to train by following international ratings, making it a smoother transition when competing in other regions. By doing specific dances at each level, dancers can be critiqued based on set criteria no matter what country they are competing in, although small regional difference do still exist.

There is also annual medal testing where judges are brought in to examine dancers one-by-one, as well as grade their knowledge of Highland dance in a theory test. At each level they are rewarded a medal starting with pre-bronze and reaching gold, then onto the Scottish Award, which goes up to level five. From there, dancers can do their Associates Certificate, allowing them to teach, and then study for the hardest level of all, becoming a judge.

"That's a really hard one because you have to know *everything*," Jasmin tells me while we sit down for a chat with her mother. "You're judging people who could be doing any different step [from their particular region]; they're like different styles of Highland dancing, there are little differences. So you have to know the differences between the two styles and you have to be able to recognize all the steps and all the problems in the steps, because if you're judging a competition, you have to know *everything*."

Her mom jumps in: "And just like, *So You Think You Can Dance*, certain judges have certain preferences within that range. So that's where you get the variation in a decision as to whether one dancer might be rated ahead of another. It's the judges' personal preference that comes into play, but they're still doing things officially, by the book. You can see that, the variation from time to time where you have one judge who judges the dancer and if there are three judges at championships – we were in Toronto for Canadians [competition] and they had judges that moved. They moved so [the competitors are] being judged by different judges. So one judge might rate them higher than another judge who's judging them for the same dance. But they move the judges around so they don't have one judge judging the same dancer."

The intensity that competitors approach Highland dancing with doesn't end there, though. Barb Murray of Barb Murray's School of Highland Dance in Fredericton (the first school and now one of two in the city) is even more serious, well, serious in a Scottish, fun-loving sort of way.

Although the dance season usually goes from September to June, Barb says, "I don't stop. I left a full time job to do this, so I don't stop. And I also find, too, that the kids lose too much when they're gone… A lot of kids have personal trainers now. They work on different muscle groups. It is very, very serious. They're extremely athletic. I played a lot of sports at the University of Lethbridge – nothing is like Highland dancing.

"We now have sports psychologists and physiotherapists who work with us, which is really great. It's something that's been lacking in New Brunswick, the resources. We're slowly, in this area, making connections. Like, my particular school, I'm very lucky. I have two physiotherapists for dance parents. They've been given permission by the province to put together a program for the kids for stretching, to help them develop proper alignment in their legs and reduce injuries. So it's wonderful. One of my students, her great aunt is a sports psychologist. So the kids had a chance to have a session with her."

On top of the actual training, there is the travelling and the costumes. Barb tries to have the dancers compete and perform all over the world, seeing that as an important part of their training. Her studio has gone to the United States, Scotland, Ireland, France and throughout Canada. They fundraise almost all year, every year to help families deal with the financial burden, and apply for grants from the province, which are there some years and not the next. The largest grant they have been able to apply for so far is $3,000 for the whole studio.

The costumes cost almost as much as the classes themselves. "The socks that the dancers wear with the kilts cost $295 now," Barb says. But why?

"They're very, very difficult to get," usually coming from the UK. "A uniform for a dancer now costs between $1,600 and $1,800. A kilt is $800… Then they have their national costumes, and that's not quite as bad. We have parents in the city that make them, so we just have to buy the fabric. It's usually only a couple hundred dollars for that."

Talk about commitment. I remember Jasmin telling me that she didn't start buying her kilts firsthand until she had almost stopped growing because it was too expensive to buy brand new ones every year.

Probably the highest cost of all, though, is the physical injuries. I was told many times that Highland dancers have one of the highest rates of sports injuries in Canada. Jasmin has sprained both ankles and already has knee problems.

"You think of high contact sports as being football or something like that where you're actually coming in contact with other people, but this is really a high contact sport because you're always coming in contact with the ground," she explains. "There are programs developed specifically for Highland dancers because we get injured so often."

With a couple of classes per week plus solo lessons, it's a regular beating on the knees, calves, ankles and feet, always in the same repetitive manner. Some dancers also take regular ballet classes, which helps them with positioning and turn out, but also adds to the stress on their bodies.

Dancing on wood is probably the best surface because there is give to it, but often dancers must perform on concrete or, as was the case when Jasmin travelled to Brittany, cobblestones became the dance floor. "I got to dance with the pipe band as a dancer. We travelled around Brittany, France and saw a bunch of concerts and festivals, and we were always dancing on cobblestones. Our shoes had massive holes; some of us came back with really bad injuries. We'd be in a parade and we would stop in the middle of the parade and do a Celtic dance... That was pretty rough."

On the night I spoke with Barb, she was telling me about the most common injuries of Highland dancing, most frequently the Achilles tendons and plantar fasciitus because of the repeated hopping on the balls of the feet, especially in children and teenagers whose bodies are still developing.

"I had stopped competing because of an injury, which I eventually had operated on. I was only 18 when I stopped competing... A bad injury for a dancer, and it happens often, is the Achilles tendon. Actually, two years ago I cracked my heel and it rolled up part of my Achilles." The night before, which was wet and cold, she was out running around doing last minute jobs at the festival and it was enough to open up the crack again.

"If you see me on crutches tomorrow..." And true to her prediction, she was limping around the next day on crutches.

Although younger dancers seem to be getting more and more competitive, there is also a trend in older dancers competing and forming groups just for fun. People in their early twenties would rarely be seen in competitions 10 to 15 years ago, but now there is a category for those 23 years old and over. Barb thinks this prolonging of young people's dance lives is because of things like the involvement of physiotherapists, trainers and the advancement of technology for Highland shoes. You can now buy slippers with pads in them that help soften the weight on the joints.

There was even a mom and dad's Highland Fling competition in Moncton a few years ago. Most of the competitors had sons and daughters who danced, but they had never tried it for themselves. Everyone had a ball as they vied for the ultimate grand prize: a bottle of scotch.

As with any studio dancing culture, there forms a particular bond between the parent and the dancer, not unlike the "hockey dad" and his son. It's usually mothers and daughters who spend all their time after school hours organizing crammed schedules, costume fittings and the constant practising that becomes the norm.

As I sit down with Jasmin and her mother, I see that same bond that existed between my mother and I, fostered over years of time in the car together driving to practices – devouring a meal in my lap and chatting about rehearsals and studio drama – and being backstage pinning costumes and solving disasters.

One of the early tales of Jasmin's dance life includes her older sibling, a piper, as he gradually sped up his playing as the performance went on. Their mom, Alison, still gets a kick out of it: "The first time her big brother piped for her, she was dancing with a friend and they looked like two little wind up toys at the end because he was nervous and they were going around and I thought, 'Oh my God, they're going to fall over!' He said, 'I'm sorry, I just got nervous' and they kept dancing faster and faster. They were quite little at the time and he was probably only 13 or 14. It was so funny!"

Jasmin rolls her eyes.

Nerves are not only for pipers, but for dancers, too. Jasmin says that she still gets nervous, even after having been on stage for so many years.

"Sometimes I get nervous when I'm performing," she shrugs, "but normally, like, in big competitions, I get a little nervous, but a lot of the time once I'm up on stage, I don't mind so much. It's just before I go on stage I'm really nervous and I'm tense."

Alison jumps in. "And sometimes there are things that happen, like pants slitting open just before you're supposed to go up and at Canadians [competition] I had to go back, and she's in the bathroom, and I'm stitching up a seam in the pants in like three minutes before she has to compete. She's trying to focus on the steps and I'm telling myself, 'hurry up!' and she's trying not to bleed [as I poke her]! So there are things that happen. As a mother, you carry ice packs, you carry snacks, you carry sewing kits, you carry everything that you need in a container, and more. And you try to bring a gopher. We had her little brother then, so I'd say, 'Go get that!' You carry a lot of stuff with you and hopefully, you know, patience, which I'm thin with, too."

Jasmine laughs. "But I find once you're on stage, I find it much easier to block out the other people and, actually, I like dancing on stage. I just don't like the before part. It really doesn't make a whole lot of difference [if it's a big or a small crowd]. Like, there was a huge crowd at Canadians and it didn't really bother me, I just kind of don't focus on them. Sometimes it's more nerve wracking with a smaller crowd because often you know some of the people, they're a little bit closer, and you can see them. So I find it more nerve wracking when it's a smaller crowd. When it's a large crowd, they're normally just a whole bunch of faces and you can't see anyone.

"It was kind of funny, one of the girls I dance with, she was saying that she got on stage at Canadians and she's standing there, and she's like, 'All these people talk when I'm dancing.' So she starts thinking about this and she gets up on stage and she's hearing everyone talk and that's all she could hear the entire time she was dancing. So she had a really hard time focusing on that dance. After, she's like, 'I don't know why I did that.'"

Her mom shakes her head in amusement. Because Jasmin also pipes (she got injured in grade six and decided to take up piping because she couldn't dance), her poor mother had double duty some years when Jasmin competed in both.

"She did both [piping and dancing at the games] for two summers and I had a change station between the pipe field and the dance stage. And she would come off one thing, change, and go to the other. She did it for two years and then she injured herself again and we had a summer off because the physiotherapist said she should take six months off dance to give her body a rest. And it was the best summer I've had!"

We continue to chat about competitions, practices and costumes in one of the festival tents, pipers practicing in the nearby field and dancers walking past in their Highland garb. I watch Jasmin and Alison's casual behaviour with each other and see my mom and I in their continuous banter and the eye rolls that Jasmin does frequently when her mom tells stories about her. We talk for almost an hour about Highland dancing, yet the conversation is about so much more than dance.

CANADA

QUEBEC

Montreal

USA

4 Quebec: Contorting in the Cirque du Soleil

I remember being quite impressed in elementary school when I heard that the Cirque du Soleil was Canadian. You mean those high-flying, spectacular trapeze artists were from my own country? How cool. Something so exotic always seemed to come from somewhere else. I never had any aspirations to join the circus, as my dance classes clearly taught me that I wasn't one of the ultra flexible ones, but their world fascinated me for that very reason: I couldn't pull off what they were doing.

The story of the troupe started out on a small, seemingly insignificant stage. Although now they are known all over the world and are the largest and most successful circus, Cirque du Soleil was once just a group of young Quebec performing artists who showed off their stilt-walking, fire-breathing and juggling skills on the streets of Baie-Saint-Paul, a small town near Quebec City. It was the 80s and they called themselves Les

Échassiers Baie-Saint-Paul (the Baie-Saint-Paul Stiltwalkers), founded by Gilles Ste-Croix. Although not initially a financial success, the performers worked and toured their show, eventually breaking even.

From their modest success, a young hopeful named Guy Laliberté and the rest of the troupe created a cultural festival called La Fête foraine de Baie-Saint-Paul that offered performances and workshops for the public. This put the troupe on the map enough for the Quebec government to approve a grant for a show called Le Grand Tour, by the newly-formed Cirque du Soleil (Circus of the Sun), that was to be created for the city of Quebec's 450th anniversary celebrations of French explorer Jacques Cartier's arrival. That was the chance the group needed to catapult themselves onto the world stage.

They performed in what would become their iconic blue and yellow big top tent, seating 800 people. A tour across Canada to Vancouver's Children's Festival and Expo '86 grew their need for a tent capacity of 1,500 spectators, allowing them to head south for the first time and present their show at the Los Angeles Festival. By 1990, the troupe was performing to a 2,500 strong crowd and travelling to London and Paris, then onto Japan and other parts of Europe.

Possibly one of the most important moves for the company was their first permanent show in Las Vegas, of which there are now seven, including *The Beatles LOVE* at the Mirage. Perhaps the most ingenious of them all is the aquatic show *O* at the Bellagio, where a pool of water makes up the stage and synchronized swimmers and divers perform in and out of it. Then there was the *Superbowl XLI* performance in Miami, the permanent *Viva ELVIS* at ARIA Resort & Casino in Las Vegas, and two shows, *KÀ* and *TOTEM*, written and directed by Canadian favourite Robert Lepage. They have also taken on the first large scale show about Michael Jackson since his death in *The Immortal World Tour*.

There might not be another company with a founder as notorious as their Artistic Guide: Guy Laliberté. His reputation is one of star power, a jet setting lover of life who works just as devotedly as he parties. He is presented in the media as a ladies man who is always at the centre of attention, and as generous as he is vivacious. Regardless of his image, though, are the impressive facts of his life so far. After winning $696,220 at the World Poker Tour at the Bellagio in Las Vegas in 2007, he created the ONE DROP charitable organization a year later that aims to help provide access to water for everyone, as well as develops projects to raise awareness about the importance of universal access to water now and for future generations.

His most outrageous act was spending a reportedly $35 million to be the first Canadian space tourist. With a mission to raise awareness about water issues around the world, as well as promote Cirque's 25th anniversary, he called it a "Poetic Social Mission" and recorded a webcast with actors, activists, politicians and school children from 14 different cities reciting a poem written by Yann Martel. He spent 12 days in space.

On top of his personal undertakings, he and Cirque were honoured with a star on the Hollywood Walk of Fame in 2009. Cirque has now toured five continents for about 100 million spectators, and shows no signs of slowing down. Melena Rounis, one of the dancers in *The Beatles LOVE* show in Las Vegas, is as impressed as the rest of the world with this once-small company, and she has been working with them since 2008. Melena and I grew up dancing together at Caulfield School of Dance in Port Moody, B.C. She was always the most flexible in our group of girls, but had no intention of joining a circus company.

"I wasn't really exposed to Cirque du Soleil's work until my late teens," she tells me. "My mother and father were watching television one evening. I had just returned home from dance class and was finishing up my homework. My parents called me into the living room to come see what it was they were watching, a documentary on Cirque du Soleil. They asked me if this was something I would ever want to do. I told them, 'Yeah, sure, one day,' and went about the rest of my evening. To be honest, I was amazed by the production they put forth but didn't know if, when, where or how they would ever have room for a dancer like myself."

Her training didn't have any hint of circus in it, nor did anyone in our group consider a company like Cirque as a future employer. Being half

Greek, Melena was surrounded by other kinds of music and dance. This led to her studying jazz by the time she was 10 years old, and then adding ballet, modern and hip hop at the studio. Of course, Greek dancing was also something she learned, as well as a little bit of Chinese and Indian dance (Bhangra and Bharatanatyam).

After high school, she trained towards a BFA in contemporary dance at Simon Fraser University, covering Graham, Cunningham and Limon techniques. From there she took on more hip hop, as well as locking, popping, house, voguing, waacking and commercial dance choreography in Los Angeles and New York City. Travelling back and forth from coast to coast was challenging and unpredictable for her, but she loved every second of it.

"I learned a lot about people," she says. "A lot about what it takes, and what people think it takes [to be a dancer]… In my various trips to LA, I did it a couple different ways. There were short visits where I stayed with friends and hopped around, and there were longer visits where I would either rent a furnished apartment, preferably from a friend, or stay in a hostel.

"I must say that the Orbit [Hotel and] Hostel near Melrose and Fairfax was a great experience for me. I stayed there with one of my dear friends and we were pure entertainment to all who stayed there for our month and a half adventure. They liked us there. We would wake up usually around 11 a.m. and were in class, depending on the day, anywhere from 2 p.m. to 11 p.m.

"We danced. We would come back to the hostel like sweaty messes exhausted with big smiles on our faces and everyone would want to hear about what we did, learned and, most importantly, wanted to see what we learned (or learn a lil' somethin' themselves). We had the opportunity to perform at the *Choreographers Carnival* at the Key Club several times, at *Battle Zone* [a clowning and krumping dance competition made famous in the 2005 documentary, *Rize*], as well as meet some really inspiring individuals. They are definitely what helped keep us motivated and improving.

"In New York City I stayed with friends, as it is super expensive to find a place when travelling by yourself, though I'm sure there are reasonable ways to do it. I was fortunate enough to know some people within Manhattan, Harlem and the Heights. I learned the subway, sort of, while I travelled there but every time I went back I stayed in a different part of town, so there was definitely some adjustment time for me to figure out how to get where I wanted to go every time I visited.

"My schedule in New York was similar to my schedule in LA: wake up around 10 a.m. or 11 a.m. and take class well into the evening, meet people and be social. I definitely did more sightseeing and food tasting, though, while in New York. There are so many great little spots to try! I trained at all the major studios, Broadway Dance Center, Peridance [Capezio Center], Steps [on Broadway], with friends in their apartments, in the club – they know how to dance in New York City!"

So it seemed Melena was on course for a career in the mainstream dance world, or perhaps a spot on *So You Think You Can Dance*. Instead, "In 2005, there was an advertisement in a provincial newspaper about open call auditions for Cirque du Soleil, but they were in Las Vegas. Being as Las Vegas is the entertainment capital of the world, which is exciting, and that there wasn't too much that interested me in Vancouver going on at the time, and nothing really holding me back, I thought, hey, why not go. At worst, I will have a vacation in Las Vegas.

"I decided to go try my luck and, to my surprise, after two FULL eight to nine hour days of auditioning, I made it to the end of the audition process and was put on file. The show they had me in mind for (*The Beatles LOVE*) was five months into creation already and there were no more contracts available at the time. They told me that those contracts were up for renewal in two years and that at that point I may hear something."

Not one to wait around for someone else to call, Melena stayed in Vancouver and opened a dance studio on Commercial Drive, called the Drive Dance Centre, with her business partner Geneen Georgiev in 2007. (It's now one of the best drop in dance centres in the city.) But as John

Lennon once said, life is what happens to you while you're busy making other plans.

"I got a call from Cirque [almost a full two years after my audition] stating that I was a potential candidate for a position in *The Beatles LOVE* in the Mirage Hotel and Casino in Las Vegas. It was late October and they were curious as to my availability. Being a new business owner, this call made me very nervous, but understanding what a life changing experience this would be, made my nervousness turn to excitement. They were definitely concerned that I had just opened up a business but I assured casting that the studio wouldn't be an issue and let them know I was interested and available.

"They told me there were just several other auditions that needed to take place before they could confirm I had the job. I asked where, so that I could have a bit of an idea what I was up against, and they told me Toronto, New York, Chicago and possibly Europe. I was stunned. That many other places? That many more people? I didn't know what to say so I wished them luck and hung up the phone thinking, well, that was the biggest, fastest high and low I had ever experienced in a matter of minutes.

"In January 2008 I received another call from casting informing me that they were through auditioning folks and that I got the job. My family and business partner were very understanding and encouraging and we decided that this was a once in a lifetime experience I had to have." A couple of months later and she was in Montréal at Cirque headquarters for intensive preparation.

"We trained Monday through Friday for two weeks, 9 a.m. to 5 p.m., sometimes 6 p.m. In that time we would have gum booting class with a brilliant man from South Africa that was brought all the way to Montréal to educate us on the style of dance and history of its origin. Stomping our feet in rhythm with his and learning his percussion patterns was how we would start the morning at 9 a.m. for roughly one hour. I would barely be awake at this point and he would be shouting 'with more energy!' in his South African accent. It was priceless.

"We would then learn choreography from the show, go for strength testing and training to make sure we were fit and healthy to do 10 shows a week with no potential risks, and go to costume fittings and measurements. We even had plaster moulds taken of our heads so that they would have the correct sizing and measurements to create our head pieces accurately. I was able to re-choreograph sections of the show where I was featured to better suit my style, we got a sneak peak at what they were creating for *Zed* in Japan and we even got in a couple days of sightseeing."

Training was different and yet the same as her regular dance show preparation. "Given the fact that I was being integrated into an already fully functional show," Melena says, "the initial training was the same as it would be for any major production that is already up and running. There were many elements and things to learn about in a condensed period of time, which made it challenging, yet exciting.

"I was taught how to properly hang in a harness, as well as use a swivel harness while automation moved me up and down and in and out of the space on stage, which was new to me, and the importance of working out or conditioning outside of my discipline. I became much more aware of my surroundings at all times and the importance of continuity in my choreography and blocking on a daily basis.

"I witnessed the artists training for other shows in Montréal, which was inspiring, but I didn't have a full grasp of what Cirque would be like for me until I was surrounded by my fellow cast members at *LOVE*. The true difference between being a dancer and a Cirque performer wasn't fully comprehensible for me until we got to Las Vegas.

"I think the most unique part about working for Cirque is the company's ability to combine so many different skills, talents, specialties, ethnicities, cultures and heritages under one roof into an hour and a half production. It's amazing."

By April, Melena had moved to Vegas and rehearsals at the Mirage started in full swing. It was a condensed schedule of long days. "It was completely different trying to figure everything out on the stage. The *LOVE* theatre sits in the round so just navigating your way in the space was challenging, let alone the fact that the stage is powered by hydraulics and it moves in pieces with a top speed of a foot a second. We quickly learned the importance of knowing where you are going at all times and always taking the same pathway at all times.

"We had two weeks worth of staging and rehearsals on stage before we actually went into the show and were integrated slowly, several acts or cues at a time until we knew and were comfortable with the whole show. We watched the show at least 10 times and shadowed the artists we were replacing. It all went very smoothly."

Melena was performing by May and settled into life with Cirque, where she still works. "Years later, rehearsals are roughly the same as when we first integrated. As the cast continues to grow and change over it is truly a never-ending integration process, which can become wearing on anyone given the amount of times we have had to integrate someone into the show because they are new or returning back after an absence.

"The most valuable things that I learned joining Cirque don't necessarily apply to my art as much as they do to my day-to-day appreciation for life, and an opportunity such as this.

"On a daily basis we are surrounded by a plethora of languages – German, French, Portuguese, Russian, Romanian, Spanish, English, Swedish, Zulu, British and Australian slang – I could go on! We get to experience different cultural holidays, foods, traditions, words, sayings and so much more that makes this experience so beautiful and like no other.

"To me these differences in themselves are the tools we have gained and are what unite us as a cast and in some ways as a family. They have helped build and form Cirque's reputation and internationally acclaimed success, and are one of the reasons you cannot duplicate a production company such as theirs. We all have such a great appreciation and admiration not only for each other's abilities and work ethics, but for who each and every one of us is and where we come from."

That camaraderie also makes the demanding show schedule easier to handle. Melena goes into the theatre on work days at around 3 p.m. or 4 p.m., but sometimes as early as 1:30 p.m. for training or staging. She then does a half an hour of Pilates, a strength training session with one of their personal trainers or a 25-minute run on the treadmill, and some physical therapy. Make up is about a 50-minute chore, although she has now gotten it down to around half an hour if need be.

The show itself is an hour and a half maximum, as per Las Vegas casino rules, and then she stretches and does preventative icing before heading home at about midnight, five days a week, "just like any other job." Although contracts are signed on a yearly basis, about a third of the cast has remained the same since the beginning. The turnover is mostly with the children, as they need six boys to work a maximum of four days a week (eight shows) for the "Kids of Liverpool" section. These children are privately schooled by Cirque and help keep the atmosphere light behind the scenes.

As for Melena, you can see her on stage right from the beginning of the show. "I believe my character name is Baby in Black and I mainly wear the rainbow leg warmers and arrow print jumper with the blue head-band," she smiles.

"I can usually be found straight away in the top of the show performing to 'Get Back,' as well as locking on top of the VW Beetle we have on stage during 'Drive My Car,' if I'm not flying in the 'Something' act. I am also one of the falling heads in 'Mr. Kite.' I play a groupie who is so intoxicated that her head keeps falling off… It's quite brilliant.

"During the 'Peace and Love' section of the show I can sometimes be seen as a jellyfish in 'Octopus's Garden' and in 'Lady Madonna' or 'Come Together,' provided I'm not performing as Lady Madonna that evening. Ultimately our roles, as you can see, rotate and we essentially all understudy each other's spots to a certain degree. It is useful for the company and it helps keep us stimulated."

Some of the remarkable opportunities that working for Cirque has given Melena also keep her stimulated. Among them was "escorting Sir Paul McCartney, Yoko Ono and Olivia Harrison on stage at the five year anniversary of *LOVE* in front of a packed house filled with friends, family and celebrities. "It was a pretty surreal experience."

A lot of performers who aspire to do what Melena is doing with Cirque go the more traditional route and attend the National Circus School in Montréal. The school's preparatory program starts 9-13 year olds with 13 hours per week of training to begin their career. For those in high school, they can enrol in both circus arts training and regular curriculum school, finishing with a high school diploma. There are even dormitories for out of town students and those who want to live there for a fully integrated period of training. For those who have already completed high school, there are higher education programs that lead to circus arts diplomas.

Across the country, staff travel to about 20 cities scouting talent on a pre-selection tour every year. Those auditioning, between the ages of 9 and 17, go through workshops to test their "spatial orientation, coordination, flexibility, strength, stage presence (acting ability), movement and musicality (dance)," I'm told. As well, annual entrance exams in Montréal, Toronto, Vancouver and Paris assess even more in depth those same skills before staff choose the students they will accept that year.

My stint in the life of a training circus artist brings me to the school in Montréal to get a sneak peek at what they are doing. I step off the bus on Jarry Street and walk along Second Avenue. The late September day is cool but a sky full of sunshine lends the air a pleasant crispness as I cross the street and see the building: layer upon layer of rectangular windows make up the 10-storey glass box that looks attached to the existing structure like a false front western town façade.

A huge front lawn is littered with skinny trees, mismatched bikes, baby strollers and parents, the kids showing off their best circus performer moves on top of the blue mats thrown over the grass. It's like a picnic gone wild, with impromptu cheering and small bodies flying through the air; the only thing missing is a basket of homemade sandwiches and a red- and white-chequered cloth to sit on.

Today the school is open to the public as part of Journées de la Culture, a province wide cultural weekend that now spans across Canada and sees free activities put on by cultural organizations and artists. Students are in-studio doing workshops, training and performing excerpts of shows, while the public filters in and out of the maze of rooms as they please.

As I step inside the front door I am greeted by a female clown dressed in a white and red spotted ruffled top and tights. Her painted face, white with exaggerated lips and cheeks, her eyes wide as spotlights, plays like a silent film of expressions as she stares at me, giggles, says "hello" and shyly pinches my nose. I can't help but laugh and she snorts gleefully before waddling off to pinch some other unsuspecting visitor.

Taking off my scarf and draping my jacket over my arm, I scan the crowd in disbelief: students are bringing their characters out of the studios and into the hallways where they can interact with the public. A young man wearing clunky shoes, pants four sizes too large, suspenders and a shabby brown t-shirt winks at me as he walks by juggling colourful balls; a short-haired blond bends backwards into a bridge, flips her legs over her head and then continues down the hallway; teenagers congregate in groups along the outskirts, jeering and cheering on their friends who go to school here.

Making my way past studios with trapeze artists, dancers and people inside hoola hoops, all training with the doors open, I sneak into a small studio where a musical theatre-type class is going on. The teacher tells me to jump in, which I gladly do, and end up flinging my limbs all over the place while trying to sing a song I don't know the words to. The group takes it easy on me, though, and allows me to tag along for the next 10 minutes.

Once the class is over, the teacher approaches me to ask if I will be sticking around for the day. I make the mistake of saying that I came to watch some of the "real circus-y" performers train and he looks at me amused.

"And this class isn't 'real circus-y'?"

"Well, of course it is," I stammer, feeling like a cartoon character caught with her pants down in the circus ring. "I just mean the acrobatic stuff that you see in Cirque du Soleil."

"Ah," he sighs with a shake of his head, clearly having been in this situation before, "except, they can't be sought-after performers unless they're well-rounded. All of the classes here are equally important to their training, not just the flying trapeze and tightrope tricks."

Of course he's right. Just because you play right wing doesn't mean you don't have to learn how to skate backwards like a defenseman. He's a good man, though, this teacher, and he gives me a wink. "If you head down the hall to the right, the seniors are performing excerpts from a piece they're working on, probably more what you were expecting."

I give him an embarrassed smile and thank him for letting me join in on his class. "It was really fun," I make sure to reiterate, and walk quickly down the hall to the right.

Here there is an eager audience of parents, friends, neighbours, family and other students gathered at the back of the room. This studio is like a prettified warehouse space with ceilings up to the sky, windows that scale one side just as high, and contraptions coming from every which way, whether it is ribbons of cloth hanging from the ceiling or equipment pullies attached to the ground that look like they're strong enough to lift blocks of concrete, not tiny circus artists.

I join the other students who have a front row seat on blue practice mats and sit cross legged among those sprawled out in many interesting positions. We are introduced to a young woman who is in her last year of training here. Dressed in plain brown leggings and a white tank top, she walks out calmly and smiles confidently to the audience. Down comes a hoop held by two pieces of what looks like rope hanging from the ceiling. She takes the hoop in her hands and gracefully sits down like it's a swing set.

The music starts and she flips herself around as the hoop is pulled higher off the ground, her legs splitting effortlessly as her head dips upside down and she curls her legs back in as if she is crossing them to sit down for tea.

In and out of the hoop she swivels, ripples, dangles, finally reaching the ground as she pulls the hoop down and lifts herself back into it, swinging nonchalantly and barely out of breath. The aerial tricks start up again as she uses the hoop like a ballerina uses her partner, as a sturdy guide, but not as a replacement for her strength. I get the feeling that this student could be 100 feet in the air or barely off the ground and she would continue to exude a calm grace that flows from one movement to the other without a jerk or misplaced twitch. I would see even more of this effortlessness later tonight.

The National Circus School and the Cirque du Soleil headquarters assemble together in one area called La TOHU. It was created in 2004 by En Piste (the national association of circus arts), the National Circus School and Cirque du Soleil in order to put the city on the map as an international circus arts capital. What it has become is one of the "largest gathering places for circus arts training, creation, production and performance" in the world, according to its own literature. It was initially called Cité des arts du cirque, which is apt for the space it takes up.

Not set on just any plot of land, La TOHU belongs to the disadvantaged Saint-Michel neighbourhood, using staff from the area to work in the complex (especially youth who need work experience), and offers free programming to nearby residents so that the neighbourhood benefits from a cultural richness.

On the border is the Saint-Michel Environmental Complex, once a limestone quarry and one of the largest urban landfills in North America. It's now an important park space for the community and the city. The site also houses a recovery centre where city recyclables are processed, a power station that creates electricity from the biogas produced at the landfill site, and composting sites.

La TOHU is in charge of designing and presenting ecology programming on the site (which will eventually encompass all 192 hectares, almost as large as the city's glorious Mount Royal Park). There are cultural shows and environmental education programs, free activities, walking and cycling paths, cross-country skiing and snowshoeing trails, multimedia exhibitions and even guided tours.

Front and centre of the site is the Pavilion, where I go to see a show called *Le Fil sous la neige*. Apparently, this is the first circular performance hall in Canada specifically built for circus arts, and the building is remarkable. As I walk through the reception hall in the lobby, I notice a glass window in the middle of the floor. Interesting, I think, as I walk over and peer down. This is an ice bunker that acts as an air conditioner in the summer by keeping a liquid antifreeze called glycol below freezing point and turning the water inside to ice, requiring very little energy and without emitting greenhouse gases.

I also take a wander through the art exhibit covering the walls in the corner, and walk by a short trapeze wire for audience members to try out a few metres off the ground. (Note to self: come back and try it out after the show.)

Le Fil sous la neige comes all the way from France by a troupe called Les Colporteurs, who have been touring the show for a couple of years. The director, Antoine Rigot, an acrobat and tight-wire artist – who worked with Cirque in the 80s – was in a surfing accident in 2000 that left him paralyzed from the pectorals down. 10 years later, he is back in the circus, this time as the director, creating a show that fuses the poetry of dance with the intimacy of an autobiography, as the seven tightrope artists explore fragility, courage and love.

The main platform is set up on the circle stage below with ascending seats looking down as if in an indoor amphitheatre (but about a thousand times smaller). Wires crisscross at varying heights across the stage, creating a curious set. As I make my way to my seat in the fourth row, I hear a young boy ask his father in French, "But how will they get from one to the other?" His incredulousness is warranted and I try to imagine climbing from one wire to the next, let alone doing it with a partner or in a group, to music, and gracefully on my feet.

The lights go down and a man's voice is heard. This is Antoine Rigot, beginning the show with the ability that he could share, his voice. He fades to the background as the performers approach their wires and the musicians begin to play. Jumping on and off, dancing across and partnering like a ballet on tightropes, pushes the notion of what the body is capable of. Antoine's partner, Agathe, walks across a wire thin enough to slide under a doorway, in shiny purple stiletto heels, teasing the audience as she flings them off and puts them back on to continue walking; a young Finnish woman with red hair, porcelain skin and a red fairy-like skirt dons a pair of point shoes and walks across the wire *en pointe*. And then does it blindfolded.

I can feel my mouth getting dry from hanging open in disbelief since the start of the show, but none of the tricks are done for the sole purpose of applause; each tightrope artist is more concerned with the dance quality of their movements than by hamming up technique that is strong enough to last the full hour and a half. We get a deeper, more thoughtful experience and when Antoine returns to the stage to speak the epilogue, limping but walking on his own, there are tears running down my face and the row of people around me are all sharing tissues with each other. No one stays sitting in their seats when the applause starts and wave upon wave of admiration is thrown back to the creator and the tightrope artists who penetrated each and every one of us, taking us into another world.

As Antoine is quoted in the program: *"Quand nous dansons sur lui, il vibre. Cette vibration est le passeur entre le funambule et le public. C'est notre language, il est terriblement fragile, il flirte avec l'impossible, peut-être un passage entre rêve et réalité, c'est le jeu de l'équilibre, c'est le langage du funambule."*

The circus is much more than clowns and tricks, dramatic make up and flexible bodies; it has a way of breaking through more deeply than an audience expects, sometimes while they laugh, sometimes while they cry, and schools like the National Circus School and organizations like La TOHU inspire young artists to be good enough for companies like Cirque du Soleil and Les Colporteurs.

After filing out of the theatre, I head straight over to the small piece of tightrope I saw on my way in. There are already two children trying it out, to the delight of their father who stands to one side of the wire, just in case one of them falls. First the little girl steps up, no more than 10 years old, and is able to take about three full steps before falling off with a laugh. Her younger brother very seriously follows suit, concentrating on the wire like it might jump out at him, intent on doing better than his big sister. He manages two steps and then tries for a slight jump, but can't land it and falls to the ground, disappointed but still laughing.

They both encourage their dad to try it as I approach, and he is happy to oblige. Stepping onto the wire, he stops and wavers for a few seconds before having to jump off. He, too, is laughing as his children clap wildly for his attempt.

Now the tightrope is open for me and by now there is a small crowd gathered and a line up forming behind me. Never having dreamed of getting up on a piece of wire before, I'm a bit apprehensive that I'll fall and break my neck, leaving these wonderful people around me to call an ambulance and take me to hospital.

I test the tightrope out with my right foot and notice how little space it takes up underneath my shoe. I try to angle myself so that as much surface as possible is sitting on top of the wire. My left foot scoots forward and I can feel my whole balance shift uncontrollably to the right and I quickly try to even it out by taking a shaky step forward on my left foot. My arms flailing outwards trying to grasp at the unhelpful air around me, I manage one last quick step on my right foot before teetering off to the ground. My "audience" claps like I've just done a jeté on the wire and landed with grace.

On and on it goes as each new person steps up and tries to emulate even a hint of what the artists did tonight in their performance, most barely getting up before falling down, but always laughing at their attempt.

CANADA

MANITOBA

ONTARIO

Winnipeg

USA

Manitoulin
Island

5 Ontario and Manitoba: Jingling through the Pow Wow Circuit

The sun is glowing down on the Wikwemikong Indian Reserve (the only officially recognized unceded reserve in Canada) on Manitoulin Island where I am spending the weekend at a pow wow. It's the perfect temperature for an outdoor event, warm enough for the sun to burn my skin in a couple of hours, but not hot enough that my pores are constantly erupting with sweat.

At the 49th annual Wikwemikong Cultural Festival, the theme is "Honouring the growth of our children." I sit cross-legged on the grass in front of the bleachers that surround the outdoor dance circle, hanging out with mostly children, some wearing regalia, some in regular clothes.

Looking across the large circular grass area, with tiered bleachers all around except for the stage area where the MC and judges sit, I watch as women make their way into the centre. They are all wearing dresses of varying bright colours. Their skirts are lined horizontally with shiny little zigzagging cones that bump against each other, creating a shimmering melody as they walk. These jingle dresses are considered healing, the triangular-shaped cones attracting the sun and reflecting it back to the earth. As one of the stories goes:

> *A medicine man's granddaughter was very ill. He had a dream in which a spirit wearing the jingle dress came to him and told him to make one of these dresses and put it on his granddaughter to cure her. When he awoke, he and his wife proceeded to assemble the dress as described by the spirit of his dream. When finished, they and others brought his granddaughter to the dance hall and she put on the dress. During the first circle around the room, she needed to be carried. During the second circle around the room, she could barely walk and needed the assistance of several women. The third circle around the room she found she could walk without assistance and during the fourth circle around the room, she danced.*
> - Manito Ahbee: A Festival for All Nations

The women who wear jingle dresses traditionally would have fasted and feasted in order to honour the transformational powers of the dresses. Although the responsibilities associated with this ritual are not as strictly held today, dancers still feel privileged to wear their jingles at pow wows.

The energetic MC, Alex Fox, announces that girls aged 13 to 17 are now competing in the jingle dress category. The host drums, a group of men gathered in a circle to provide the songs throughout the pow wow, begin drumming and singing. The children I'm sitting with on the grass pause from playing among themselves and look up at the dancers.

Some women are competing in the traditional style, with low to the ground footwork, feet in parallel, zigzagging across the grass to represent the journey of life. They don't cross their feet, dance backwards or do full turns. The contemporary dancers are easy to spot because they lift up their knees while they zigzag, dancing backwards, turning and crossing their feet. They carry a fan that is solemnly raised up on the honour beats, a point in the song where the rhythm slows down for a few seconds. While the traditional style is grounded and calm, the contemporary style is showier and up tempo, perhaps a reflection of the differences between the older and younger generations.

The drummers bang out their last beat of the song and the girls all stop in time with both feet on the ground. Obviously pleased, the MC shouts, "How can we judge that, when dancers are dancing from the heart?" But judge them they must. Each dancer registers before the pow wow begins in their respective dance style and wears a number to identify them. At Wikwemikong, females compete in the fancy shawl, northern traditional, jingle dress and smoke dance, from the tiny tots (those who can barely walk) to the golden age (50 years old plus), while men compete in the grass dance, northern traditional, fancy dance and smoke dance.

My attention is taken away from the dance floor as one of the little girls sitting beside me tugs at my arm a few times and tells me she needs to go to the washroom. Now. She is probably five years old and clearly wants ME to take her. I hesitate, looking around for her parents or family, not knowing anyone in the crowd, but there doesn't seem to be any relatives around. I just met the child less than an hour ago, so I tell her I probably shouldn't walk away with her. There are rules against that sort of thing, you know. (I picture sirens going off and police running through the dance circle with guns drawn, knocking at the door of the outhouse, yelling at me to come out with my hands up.)

She just stares at me blankly, now shifting her weight from one foot to the other. I hesitate some more. Looking to my left, I hear a young woman laughing. "I think it's too late." I make eye contact with the little girl, whose eyes are slightly glazed over and concentrating, and realize she is doing what she needs to do right in front of me. In fact, right in front of the filled bleachers behind me, too. And it's not trickling down her leg, so I know the damage is even more unpleasant.

I look back at the young woman sitting nearby and say, half jokingly, 'Well, I guess no one will mind if I take her to get cleaned up, right?" She just shrugs good-naturedly and smiles. It's clearly my responsibility, since I'm the closest one.

So I take the girl's hand and we make our way to the nearest porta-pottie. She's not embarrassed, just happy to have a new friend. After some scrubbing and lots of disinfectant I carry in my purse, she's ready to get back out there and continue with the day. Of course, the lesson learned here is all mine: in First Nations cultures, people take care of one another, especially children, because, as well as being the responsibility of their parents, they are also the responsibility of the community as a whole. (In other words, I should have just taken her when she asked me to.)

The teen boy's fancy dance has just started as we make our way back from the porta-pottie. Brightly coloured regalia is swirling around almost frenetically as the guys show off the most athletic and high paced of the competition dances. The men's fancy isn't about history, it's about entertainment. Originating in the southern United States, it is a possible spin off of the war dance when both Canadian and American governments banned a lot of the traditional First Nations dances. The fancy was the only one allowed to be performed.

> *When the "Wild West Shows" were popular in the early 1900s, some featured Indian dancing, but the traditional and grass dance styles were considered too sedate. So the young dancers began to dress a little differently and to dance in a faster manner. Along with the new dance style came new songs.*
> - Manito Ahbee: A Festival for All Nations

This style relies on the dancer to explode with energy for the entire song, thrusting his knees up high, leaping up and down from the ground, and never losing rhythm with the rapid beats. On top of his flashy style, his extravagant regalia punctuates each movement with more emphasis. Every dancer wears a roach, which is a headdress made from porcupine quills and deer hair, and will have eagle feathers or an elaborate design that shoots out feathers from all angles. On their chest and back are matching aprons and a cape, which is fully beaded and made of cloth or ribbon.

Most characteristic of all are the two bustles they wear on their backs. Most of them that I see, especially in the younger categories, are made out of manmade feathers, died florescent colours to match the rest of their regalia, although some bustles are made of eagle feathers. Matching arm bustles give the outfit a frenetic appearance when they dance. In their hands they hold sticks covered with more feathers and ribbons, all equally bright; on their legs they wear moccasins, fur and bells that add to the effect. When it's time to clap, they often shake their ankle bells instead of clapping their hands.

Watching these guys exert so much energy is exhausting, so I decide to take a break from all the dancing and go for a stroll. Along the way I meet Dawn Madahbee, an Ojibway dancer from Birch Island who is interested that I have come all this way to learn about First Nations dancing. It isn't the cultural aspect, though, that she wants to tell me about. "The earth's core is special here," she says in her soft spoken voice. "I don't know the scientific terms, they wrote about it in the local paper, but there's something about the earth here. If you have the chance, walk around barefoot."

I take her advice and spend the next half an hour ambling around in the sunshine with my sandals in my hand. The magic must have seeped through my feet, too, because as I walk back into the bleacher area, the MC is announcing that it's time for the intertribal dance, which means the audience can participate, too. Held a few times each day, the intertribal must be danced by all of the competitors, so dancers that can barely stand on their own, smiling parents holding them up, teenagers in small groups and elders in full regalia all mix together with family and friends – First Nations and non-First Nations – and audience members who might never have been to a pow wow before.

I join the bobbing, striking mass of colour, multiple generations deep, as we slowly make our way around the circle, the drummers banging each beat with their drums and filling in the song with their voices. Still with bare feet, I follow the dancers in regalia as they bob their whole bodies to the beat with each step. I copy feet positioning, arm postures, head movements, anything to give me an idea of *how* to do this type of dance.

Yet, everyone else looks casual, like they aren't aware they are even dancing. And that is the key: I started dancing in a studio before even going to preschool, so I learned structure, self-discipline and how to follow instructions throughout a dance class. First Nations dancing isn't about structure, self-discipline and following instructions, it is about following the drumbeat with your body, about opening yourself to more than the movements you are doing. When I stop copying and just let the beats breathe through my skin, I bob along just like everyone else. Of course, I have no proof that I look natural, so you'll just have to take my word for it.

The next morning I am delighted to find out that it is time for the tiny tots (those under five years old) to compete. Some of these little ones can't even form sentences, but are dressed in traditional regalia and brought into the dance circle. Mothers hold their young one's hands as the music starts and the little girls and boys begin moving to the drumbeats. Some just look around at all the people and activity, while others keep in time naturally. Other than when the elders dance, these tiny tots garner the most cheers for their efforts and even go home with a $5 bill each.

Their older brothers and sisters, most of whom would also have competed when they were under five, are getting ready to be called up next. I love seeing the regalia of these five to seven year olds because they really bridge the gap between traditional and modern, First Nations and pop culture. Along with handmade beadwork and designs are incorporated Superman logos on the back for boys and Dora the Explorer for girls. They walk around oblivious to their representation of old and new, of traditional ways and the non-native culture their parents and grandparents had no choice but to adopt. To them, going to a pow wow during the day and then returning home to watch cartoons is normal because that's all they know, but their grandparents fought hard to preserve their land and their traditional ways.

This area, Manitoulin Island, has been populated by the Odawa people since the 1600s, although archaeological finds from the Paleo-Indian and Archaic cultural stages (the first and second periods of human occupation in the Americas, as proposed by archaeologists Gordon

Willey and Philip Phillips) date habitation as far back as 10,000 AD or earlier. In the 17th century, the Iroquois stepped in to try to control the fur trade that had been set up by the French. In doing so, they drove out the population, leaving the island uninhabited by people until the 19th century.

By the 1830s, a few Pottawatomi families had settled in Wikwemikong, and then the Ojibway arrived in the 1850s, most tribes coming from l'Arbre Croche, north of Grand Traverse Bay in Michigan. The Odawa (Ottawa) people also returned and these three tribes, the Ojibway, Odawa and Pottawatomi, formed what is called the Three Fires Confederacy.

As new settlers came in larger numbers by the late 18th and early 19th centuries, land became more coveted. The aboriginal people had started to depend on the gifts and symbolic payments that came from the government with treaty signings and grew more impoverished as the usual wildlife they depended on was depleted by the new immigrants.

A report was undertaken by Major General H.C. Darling, military secretary to the governor general in 1828, to look into the "Indian conditions" in Canada. From there a "civilization program" was shaped, recommending that the aboriginal people be put in fixed locations in order to educate them, convert them to Christianity and transform them into farmers. This led to the residential school system that was imposed upon the aboriginal people, including the Inuit in the North being shipped off of the land and put into newly formed camps.

In 1836, the Bond Head Treaty was signed, giving Manitoulin Island a refuge status for First Nations people. The government hoped that this would spur migration of Upper Canada Indians to Manitoulin Island, where they were promised they could keep their traditional way of doing things and not be influenced by the Europeans who were settling nearby. But the migration didn't happen, so the government decided to divide the islands to create both new reserves and non-native settlements; they took over any unsold land under the MacDougall Treaty of 1862.

The Chief here refused to sign the treaty, leaving an area of the island unceded. The bands of this eastern part amalgamated in 1968 to form Wikwemikong Unceded Indian Reserve, which is still what it is called today. The people of Wiky are proud that they have retained their land on their own terms.

First Nations people have been legislated by the federal government since the Indian Act was created in 1876. This act sought to define who an "Indian" was, regulate almost every aspect of their daily lives and defined what penalties they had to submit to if they broke any of the new laws. As reported by the Royal Commission on Aboriginal Peoples in 1996, it kept most who lived on reserves from voting in "federal elections until 1960. Indian people could not manage their own reserve lands or money and were under the supervision of federally appointed Indian agents whose job it was to ensure that policies developed in Ottawa were carried out on the various reserves across Canada."

Of course, First Nations were reluctant to obey these new rules. This was blamed on "the Indian mind [being] in general slow to accept improvements," but that "it would be premature to conclude that the bands are averse to the elective principle, because they are backward in perceiving the privileges which it confers," wrote Deputy Superintendent Spragge, two years after the implementation of an elective band council in 1869.

The natives were officially seen as an incompetent population who needed to be provided with education, a new religion and agricultural skills in order to live alongside the immigrants, who thought themselves superior.

As stated in the Annual Report for the Department of the Interior in 1877, "Our Indian legislation generally rests on the principle, that the aborigines are to be kept in a condition of tutelage and treated as wards or children of the State... the true interests of the aborigines and of the State alike require that every effort should be made to aid the Red man in lifting himself out of his condition of tutelage and dependence, and that is clearly our wisdom and our duty, through education and every other means, to prepare him for a higher civilization by encouraging him to assume the privileges and responsibilities of full citizenship."

In a clear demonstration of misunderstanding the culture, the deputy superintendent general Duncan Campbell Scott wrote to western official W.M. Graham in 1921 to say, "It has always been clear to me that the Indians must have some sort of recreation, and if our agents would endeavour to substitute reasonable amusements for this senseless drumming and dancing, it would be a great assistance."

The pow wow that I'm attending first started in 1860 and is one of the longest running in central Canada, no doubt due to its location on an unceded reserve. It's come a long way from the years when dancing was banned and is now a full cultural festival. The weekend includes the competition pow wow, vendors selling handcrafts, food stalls, workshops and art shows. As much as the neighbouring nations, and those from all over North America, use this time to catch up and socialize, they also provide a very welcoming atmosphere to those who want to experience a pow wow for the first time.

First Nations culture is on the mend now, as tribes turn to their elders to help them remember the old ways. Most importantly, pow wows bring together nations from all over the surrounding regions to sing, dance, drum and pass those traditions down to the next generation, who grow up with almost no First Nations education.

Pow wows also allow people like me, who are interested in learning about the people who were here before my ancestors were, to step inside some of the traditions that make up their society. Understandably, many of these traditions are closed off to the public (potlatches, for example), but pow wows are generally open to everyone and visitors are encouraged to attend.

On the Sunday that weekend in Wiky, just before 1:45 in the afternoon, the little girl I had met earlier comes to find me. She takes my hand and brings me to an older friend of hers, or maybe it is her aunt, who tells me it's time for the spectators dance competition. She gives me a feathered and beaded hairpiece and a blue satin cape with long fringes dangling down; in my hands she places a fan made of more feathers, components of the women's traditional regalia.

The little girl smiles up at me approvingly as I make my way to the dance circle. The drum beats start as they always do and my new friend starts bouncing to the rhythm. I must admit, wearing a bit of regalia somehow helps me to understand the movements better. We make our way around the circular space with smiles on our faces as others are doing the same thing. Swirling around me are brightly coloured fringes, long shimmering capes and feather bustles weaving in and out of jeans, running shoes and summer tank tops. I start sweating as the afternoon sun seeps into my skin and my cheeks turn that rosy shade of happiness.

The drums keep pounding and they energize me to make bolder moves, to turn, to become completely intoxicated with the beat and the wailing voices of the men singing. I have no idea what I look like (I'm sure the judges remember the wild-eyed dancer spinning around to her own beat), but I feel good. The grass tickles the underside of my feet with each step and being outside on this glorious summer day brings freedom into each movement. It feels like my body is beating the drum.

And with the final whack, the song is over. I bow to no one in particular and reluctantly give back the regalia. Others are doing the same and we look around at each other, breathless and smiling, privileged to be allowed into the circle. The dancer who lent me her regalia prepares herself for the next competition and my little friend runs off to join her pals.

I decide to stroll around the grounds for awhile and over to the crafts being sold on the adjacent grass field, bringing my heartbeat to a rest, and then venture over to where the circles of drummers are set up. I stand among a small crowd surrounding the circle, peering over shoulders as eight men sit on chairs around a large drum beating it with drumsticks.

A group of singers, called Host Drums, is the main group invited to drum for the pow wow, along with other Drums (groups of singers). They are a crucial part of the weekend, as they are relied upon in case others don't show up and hold a highly respectable place in the event.

I'm told the drum is not just a beat for the dancers to follow, but the reverberation of the earth's heartbeat. It is the heartbeat that governs the movements of the dancers, the voices of the singers and the rhythm of the whole pow wow itself. The circle of the drum, and the singers and the dance circle, represent unity.

Numerous groups of drummers are set up along one side of the perimeter of the dance area, called upon one at a time to drum for the dancers. It's easy to tell whose turn it is because there is always a crowd huddled around them watching, sometimes a few people thick.

The voices of the singers are high-pitched cries that blend together in songs from generations past and other tribes who have shared their own songs. Some are ancient, while others have been recently composed; they span themes of war, society and spirituality. The songs I heard were sung in "vocables," sounds that replace the actual words of a song. When tribes shared their songs with each other, often they spoke different languages and couldn't communicate by words. This was a way of conveying the songs so that they could be passed along to others in their tribe.

Although I couldn't pick it out, there is a structure to the songs. The lead singer begins with a lead in, then the second comes in, and then the rest of the group joins, repeating what the lead has sung. This comes to an end and a second half of the song begins. Dancers have to watch out for what are called the check beats, usually drummed after the middle section, where the dancers have to "check" that they are on rhythm. Judges watch to see who falters and those who do lose points in the competition.

The least elaborate of all the dances — but also the most revered, the older women usually being the most highly respected in their tribe — is the women's traditional, which has just started as I stand near the drum circles. I see the woman who had leant me her regalia take a calm walk into the dance circle and gracefully begin to bounce to the drums. She wears a beige buckskin dress with ornate beadwork and a cape with long fringes that sway gently back and forth. She looks like a sunflower softly waving on a breezy day.

Most of the women are extremely subtle in their movements, just bouncing their knees in time to the beat and staying on the outer edge of the arena. They are being judged on their poise and grace, not fancy footwork or athletic ability, dancing out of respect for their families and friends and keeping their movements modest and simple. Some women move forward in shuffling steps clockwise around the circle, while others stay in one place, dancing more internally than for the audience. There are also the women in the southern traditional who will bow slightly at the honour beats.

The most important "rule" in women's traditional is to always have one foot grounded. This dance represents a female's earthly qualities and is probably the oldest form of dance for First Nations women. To honour that, most will carry an eagle feather fan, like the one I was leant, which they hold up on the honour beats: the drum slows down and lengthens out the rhythm in a temporary pause as another sign of respect. The women's traditional is almost solemn, the dancers finding a way to express themselves in a nearly stationary way for the entire song.

On the opposite end of the spectrum is the men's traditional, based on an old form of war dancing. The men and boys re-enact the exertion required to protect their family in battle and hunt for game to provide for their tribe. Most dancers will also imitate animals like buffalo, horses and birds throughout the song, often wearing parts of an animal in their regalia to show respect and to help embody it.

Wearing specific regalia – a beaded vest and breastplate (once used in battle as protection), a porcupine hair roach with two feathers, an apron, arm band, cuffs, choker, beaded belt and a large eagle feather bustle attached to the back of their waist – the men dance as if on a hunt, with strong, low movements. They crouch, take cover, peer around trees and get ready to pounce, all the while keeping in strict time to the drummers. Often they'll have a dancing stick or eagle wing fan, something to hold in one hand to represent their weapon.

The men's traditional can be fairly intense, as the dancers imitate tracking their prey and acting out a full narrative. They are always moving forward (never retreating) and you can follow one dancer for the whole song to learn what his story is. These two traditional categories mirror the roles that women and men once played in society.

***

In order to get a better idea of how these dance styles differed from one nation to the next, I flew west to Winnipeg a few months later for the Manito Ahbee International Competition Pow Wow at the MTS Centre downtown. It was a crispy November in Winnipeg – the coldest city of over 600,000 people in the world (said Environment Canada a few years ago) – but luckily for me, the sun shone for the full four days I was there.

Before the competition pow wow begins on the weekend, I decide to spend some time taking a workshop in First Nations hoop dancing. As an educational part of the festival that spans First Nations, Inuit and Métis topics, this component is called the Manito Ahbee Education Conference and is a chance for high school students to learn more about aboriginal heritage. The workshop I attend is run by the SummerBear Dance Troupe, founded by Barbara Nepinak, and representing Ojibway, Cree, Assiniboine and Sioux tribes. I hide out among the students at the Winnipeg Convention Centre so I can take part. They don't seem to notice.

Hoop dancer Brian Clyne starts off the hour and a half workshop with a motivating speech about following your dreams and never giving up. His own story is one of overcoming countless obstacles and finding new ways to rise back up again. His dream was to become a fireman and make a difference in people's lives, but it wasn't easy to keep that goal in focus. It was his determination to achieve this one specific ambition that pushed him to finally succeed, now working as a firefighter and training his young sons to follow his lead if they decide to.

The students are well-behaved and they perk up when Brian pulls out his hoops. He has yellow and green ones, each with four small bands around them of a white square with red on each side. He wears a matching yellow and green apron and long-sleeved shirt, black leg bands and beige moccasins, his long black hair pulled back into a pony tail. Swinging his hoops around him like they are a part of his body, he jumps up and down as he spins around in circles.

Chuck Spence and Paul Duck stand in the background drumming and singing for him, keeping the rhythm while he becomes caught up in its tempo. As the last beat is hit, Brian stops on a dime to face us, one of his hoops raised triumphantly above his head. With his chest pumping heavily, Brian looks out at us through victorious eyes. His dance was performed in order to share his culture with teenaged students, but it also stands for what he has endured throughout his life, the hurdles he has had to overcome and the faith in himself that he does not let go of.

Although nations have their own stories about the origin of the dance, I learned in Winnipeg that hoop dancing was a form of healing performed by a medicine man or spiritual leader. Because of the infinite shape of a circle, the hoops also represent how everything in life is connected by energy, that there is no beginning and no end, and that every time a dancer adds a hoop to his dance, this symbolizes another facet in the journey of life. Hoops also taught lessons to those who created their own problems and brought sickness on themselves: eventually those same struggles would return back to them.

Each dance tells a story of the creation of life, creating the shape of animals as they dance to represent honour, hunting, reverence and those who came before. Healing was a natural part of this cycle. The hoops themselves can weigh between 15 and 20 pounds, depending on how many the dancer uses and what material they make them from. Most dancers will have their hoops custom made so that they are specific to their own body.

Today, hoop dancing is performed more as a storytelling device at cultural events and at competitions where one dancer annually is awarded the title World Champion. And they are gaining recognition. A multiple World Champion winner, Nakotah La Rance, performed in Cirque du Soleil's show *Totem*. But as Brian demonstrated, hoop dancing can be about much more than a performance.

After catching his breath, he invites those interested to join him up front: he will be teaching us how to hoop dance with all the extra hoops he has brought. I jump right up there with the brave students who are looking around and trying to decide if this is a cool thing to do or not. Their friends decide it is and take out their cameras to capture the chaos.

Over my right shoulder. Over my left shoulder. Over my head. Then flip the hoops behind my head and spread them like wings. This is the eagle and one of the basic shapes that a dancer can incorporate. We try it with Chuck and Paul drumming, hopping from foot to foot while turning and trying to create the eagle. It gets pretty messy in the room as we bump into each other while swirling. The students watching take advantage of our helplessness and snap photos and take videos with their phones. Brian just smiles at us encouragingly and helps out those who are getting tangled up in their hoops. Some of us have three, some of us five, but Brian danced with 15 hoops today without missing a beat.

After that workout, I feel warmed up enough to brave the chill and walk the six blocks to the MTS Centre for the pow wow. In stark contrast to Wikwemikong's warm outdoor setting, the Manito Ahbee festival is held indoors every November in Winnipeg's downtown arena.

What the festival lacks in outdoor sunshine it makes up for in education. As well as workshops similar to the one I took on hoop dancing (there are throat singing, sash weaving, native languages, traditional medicines, residential schools history, Aztec/Mayan history, leadership and digital storytelling classes, too), it holds pow wow 101 sessions for visitors who have never been (or those who have been but want to learn more about how a pow wow works). So into the bowels of the MTS Centre and back into the classroom I walk.

In a small conference space called the MM Yearling Room, a group of eight of us eagerly find seats facing a woman and man who stand at the front. Joanne Soldier, a dancer herself, and Carl Stone, on the education conference committee, are chatting between themselves about people they have or haven't seen arrive at the arena yet, and who is supposed to be coming this year and who can't make it.

Once we have all settled in, Joanne starts things off with a peek into her weekend, telling us about waking up at the crack of dawn to get all of her regalia for the competition ready (she competes in the jingle dress category), as well as her daughter's outfits. 14 month old Waasayah Munro-Soldier is debuting this year in the tiny tots traditional category, although Joanne insists that when she is older, she will decide which style of dance she wants to compete in.

Then Joanne stops. This has clearly happened to her many times. "So I always say the number one thing is, do not call this a costume, call it 'outfit' or 'regalia'. Within the dance circle we call it a rig, 'Oh, nice rig' we'll say to each other. Costume is considered offensive because on Halloween you wear a costume, but this is expensive to make, it takes a lot of time, it takes a lot of energy. And we use our spirit names."

So what are some of the dos and don'ts of pow wows? Always ask permission before taking a photo of someone in regalia. "The majority of [dancers] are fine, but there may be the odd one who doesn't want their picture taken," advises Joanne.

The same goes with touching eagle feathers or other parts of an outfit. "I've had people come up to me and they just start grabbing my jingles; always ask for permission." It is also protocol that women who are menstruating are not allowed to be near eagle feathers, so it's best to make sure it's okay before reaching out to touch their outfits.

There are special songs throughout the pow wow, and the MC will announce when you need to stand up and remove your hats during the song. This includes the Grand Entry, a long procession where the host drums play as all dancers, staff, dignitaries, royalty, flag bearers and veterans enter the arena.

Dancers are required to participate by dancing for the entire procession (at Manito Ahbee, it lasted about 45 minutes) or they will forfeit 50 points. On Saturday when there is a dinner break, two Grand Entries will take place that day to begin the competition, one in the morning and one after dinner, making for quite the stamina builder for the dancers.

Above all, Joanne encourages visitors to get involved. "Remember you're a guest, so don't be afraid to ask questions, don't be afraid to go up to a dancer and ask them, like, if they're a fancy shawl dancer, don't be afraid to ask them, 'How did you get started?' I have people come up and ask me questions all the time. It's fine. Actually, I'm honoured that people would want to come and ask me questions, so don't be afraid.

"I know there's a lot of misconceptions in the mainstream, thinking that you're not welcome to come to a pow wow, but don't be afraid. If you're driving down the highway and you see pow wow signs, go. You're not going to be turned away; you're welcome. They might even invite you to come take part in some of the dancing. I've seen that happen. So don't be afraid to come and join in."

With that our pow wow 101 course is over and it's time to go see the dancers in action. As I pick up my things to leave, I notice Joanne getting her regalia organized in tidy plastic containers. I walk over and ask her about her jingle dress and how it was made.

Clearly pleased that I approached her, she shows me the otter tails, elk teeth and shells that contribute to her outfit. "Typically this is what a dress looks like. It's pretty heavy. This one I'd say is about five to seven pounds; I have one at home that has 400 [cones] that's almost 10 pounds. People are like, 'What about the weight?' but you don't notice it, you get used to it. And it's evolved. Typically a jingle dress dancer will have the dress, they have the leggings, moccasins; my stuff's made out of porcupine quill. My sister does it; it's her job, basically, at home. She does quill work. There are not that many people that make quillwork, so my sister's making a comeback. Even in pow wow country, everything that's old is new again and there are always little trends that go on." (I remember well the children's regalia in Wikwemikong with Dora the Explorer and Superman on them.)

Later that night I see Joanne out in the centre of the arena, competing in the adult jingle dress category. She keeps her movements simpler than some of the others, especially the younger dancers who use flashy moves and flamboyant footwork. Her hands stay at her waist and she doesn't wear any plumes in her hair. With this changing of style from old to new, jingle dress has become one of the most popular categories for young dancers.

As Carl had said earlier that morning, "The jingle dress is one of the youngest dances that we have. It's only a little over a hundred years old. And yet it's found its way across North America now. There isn't one pow wow in North America where you won't see the jingle dress."

Next up is the women's fancy shawl dance, a much less popular style to compete in, not because women don't like it, but because of its aerobic intensity. The songs are very fast, making the dancers swirl butterfly-like in their brightly coloured shawls. As with the jingle dress, the fancy shawl has seen much transformation over the years. The festival program describes its possible beginnings:

> *Although there is more than one version of the origin of Women's Fancy Dance, its evolution has been witnessed by the public in the pow wow arena. One anecdote relates that women were dancing in men's fancy dance regalia, and when they began to enter competition and beat the men, it was decided that they should have their own dance.*

Footwork is intricate and detailed; the dancers are known for their grace within the high-paced steps. A newer generation is evolving this category even more, throwing in hip hop-style moves and more decorative ways of using their shawls. The once elaborate footwork done by the older generation is being replaced with kicking up of the feet and knees, and spinning, which some judges like and some don't.

I can only imagine how difficult it is to judge pow wows, as, on top of personal style preferences, judges must give points based on the visual presentation of regalia, the dancer's style, and his or her attention to the beat. (If he or she doesn't finish on the exact ending beat of a song, they say the dancer was "bucked off" or "overstepping" and they lose points.) Judges must also keep track of all the dancers who participate in the intertribal dances, where everyone gets involved, only giving points to those who are participating.

Carl says that "You usually have to dance for a couple of years before you even place. Sometimes you see someone, though, and you're just drawn to them even if you don't know them. They look like they're floating on air. Even people who don't know the dancing are drawn to that person."

These things, although subjective, are taken very seriously by the dancers. Not only are they performing in front of elders, community members, family and friends, but they are competing for prize money. At Manito Ahbee, dancers can only compete in one category or all categories, the latter called an All Around Special.

Joanne, for example, as a jingle dress dancer, could leave with $1,200 for first place, down to $100 for sixth place. If she was entered into the All Around Special, she could win $1,200 in each category (traditional, jingle dress and fancy shawl). There is also a Women's All Around "Life Giving" Special of another $1,200. In total the year I went, over $118,000 was given out to both dancers and drummers.

These pow wows are connected to festivals all over North America, so dancers and drummers can do a circuit, competing in all of them. As much as the prize money is appealing, most dancers don't place, yet they continue to compete and have their regalia made. Being a dancer is a status to be proud of, regardless of how many competitions they have won.

It is dancing that brings together tribes from all over North America to compete against each other, to share traditional similarities and differences, and to let non-aboriginal people learn about the first cultures on this continent. The dances change over the years, reflecting new generations and their own influences, adapting the traditions of their grandparents and their grandparents' grandparents, to be able to exist in this rapidly evolving world.

There will always be the elders who shake their heads at the younger generation's behaviour and teenagers who push the boundaries of traditions that they have been taught. In dancing, though, everyone can be on the same beat, regardless of their fancy footwork or swirling shawls.

CANADA

SASKATCHEWAN

• Saskatoon

USA

6 Saskatchewan: A Fiddle Fest the Métis Way

I haven't stood in front of an audience like this since I was 17 years old. Sure, I have performed since then, but I haven't been in a competition. And I am here to vie for first, second, third or fourth place, all of which come with a cash prize.

I never meant to be here — looking out at hundreds of faces I don't know, most belonging to prairie folk seated on fold up lawn chairs under a concert-sized canopy — yet standing on the elevated stage with the stairs behind me, two fiddlers to my left and three judges behind a table in front of me, there is no escaping that I am the focus of everyone's attention.

The competition is part of the John Arcand Fiddle Fest, an annual Métis gathering on John and his wife Vicki's acreage, called Windy Acres, about seven kilometres west of Saskatoon. John is a highly revered Métis fiddler who brings together others almost as legendary as himself to teach workshops and play during the evening concerts. That is the main reason why hundreds of people pitch their tents and drive their RVs here to camp on the outer grass field that John and Vicki turn into a parking lot for the festival.

As for me, I am here for the jigging. Workshops throughout the day teach traditional Métis jigging (along with fiddling, guitar and piano) specific to the area, called the Red River Jig.

I stand upon that wooden stage, which is a simple grey box with a red fabric trim hanging around the outside. Surrounded by expectant eyes, I step into the preliminary round of the Canadian Red River Jigging Championship. The title in and of itself makes me trepidatious enough to think about walking back down the steps behind me and through the flapping canopy doorway to join the audience watching. But the thrill of plonking myself in front of an audience and doing something I have never done before this weekend is too tempting: the fiddle reminds me of my time in Cape Breton, performing takes me back to my childhood when my first step on stage was at two years old and jigging is a bit like tap dancing (and I was a fierce little tapper once upon a time). So on I go.

Wearing a pair of very untraditional khaki three quarter inch pants, a pink sports tank top and flat black shoes, I walk to the centre of the stage, nodding to the fiddlers, one of whom is about to become my partner while I jig, making eye contact with the judges, and acknowledging the audience with a smile. At this point, it's like trying to win over children in elementary school so I'm not picked last for the baseball team; I am desperate to be liked.

I wait a breath and then the first strike of the fiddler's bow collides with the strings and I let the Red River Jig tune, the most famous of all Métis tunes, soak into my feet. And then they begin moving, tapping out the basic step to the higher section of the song, matching the tune's upbeat tempo with a six-beat jig step that changes feet, the first step I learned yesterday. Then the fiddler changes rhythms and transitions into the lower section that picks up even more and challenges me to perform complex footwork that sounds like the beat of a horse's hooves. These "fancy steps" are the ones I am being judged on and after every basic section I must come up with a different fancy step until I run out. The competition is half a test of footwork and half a test of endurance.

You'll be happy to know that I made it to the finals the next day.

Back in my hotel room that night, I go over everything I have learned over the past two days, a grand total of three hours of actual Red River Jig training. In my first class, Stewart Greyeyes got down to basics by wrangling about 20 of us under the big canopy tent. A wooden floor had been installed to replace a smattering of chairs, which became our dance floor (and later the scene of the old time dances).

Stewart, in his casual blue jeans and white button up shirt, gathered us together and started the workshop by telling us, "My mother always said, still says, 'If you have two legs, you can dance.'" The next most important piece of advice? "A jigger should be able to dance on any type of floor in any type of shoes." (I think he was referring to the new form of Métis dancing where groups dress in frilly square dance costumes and jiggers wear clickers, like tap shoes, so that the audience can hear their sounds better.) At this festival, no clickers are allowed, as tradition is king. (It is wholly unlikely that jiggers would have had clickers in the 17th and 18th centuries, right?).

The six-beat basic step is the staple of the Red River Jig, gluing together the dance: step heel toe hop touch touch, repeat starting on the other foot. The step itself is easy to learn (apart from all that shortness of breath and sweating), but it's the quick rhythm that keeps your brain on high alert when you're just learning.

My last two workshops were with Yvonne Chartrand, a multi-trophy winning jigger (here and at other festivals) and one of the judges. She describes the music as crooked, sometimes on a 4/4 beat, but sometimes not; the syncopated rhythm has a distinct bounce that makes it extra jaunty. It is something I heard throughout the festival, that traditional Métis fiddlers all play the tune a bit differently and like to add in a beat or drop one out whenever it suits them. Different fiddlers also play various versions of the tune, changing from the basic to the fancy part on different counts. It is the dancer's job to listen to the phrases and let the rhythm dictate their steps. Yes, it is as hard as it sounds.

A very well-mannered fiddler played the Red River Jig for an hour straight during each workshop as we all tripped our way through the steps, clunking down on pieces of plywood boards set on top of the grass away from the main stage area. Yvonne's approach was fairly practical: as I mentioned before, the John Arcand Fiddle Fest is all about tradition, and the jigging the Métis people were doing over three hundred years ago was close to the ground, with intricate footwork and small steps, so this is what the judges here are looking to see. Another reason to keep things low and small? "To preserve your energy!" Yvonne tells us with a laugh.

From the basic step we moved onto some fancy steps. These three-count moves are faster and more intricate than the basic, always tapped out with the utmost ease (eventually). You know you're doing the steps right, in any variation, if your feet sound like galloping horses as they take off along the prairies.

Fancy steps can be in a variety of forms, although most will make the galloping sound. Yvonne taught us touch steps to the front, side and back; skipping steps (women skip forward and men skip backwards); and even some more complicated variations that took up six counts each.

We collected all of these to stockpile as big a repertoire as possible. At this festival, the Red River Jig tune is played for as long as the dancer has steps to dance, which can go on for two minutes or until the jigger has exhausted every step they know, with stories being told of over 65 steps being danced (and used up two tired fiddlers along the way). A real feat. At most other festivals, jiggers are only given time to show off three or four fancy steps before being judged.

For those competing at the John Arcand Fiddle Fest — about four of us from Yvonne's workshop competed, although I think I was the only one who hadn't planned on it — the judges give points for every fancy step executed correctly with the right rhythm, keeping low to the ground, and without moving the upper body except to bounce, much like the Cape Breton style of step dancing I learned in Nova Scotia.

One of the most common stories of how the Red River Jig came to be was that a group of Métis traders were travelling along the prairies of what is now southern Manitoba. They set up camp in a suitable creek valley that ran into the Red River and happened to be near an already-established Scottish settlement.

At night the traders heard wafts of bagpipe tunes carried across the valley to their camp, and as they sat around their own bonfire telling stories and relaxing, those pipe tunes continued to drift towards them. A Métis fiddler took out his violin and began playing to complement the pipes. Unable to help himself, another of the men stood up and began jigging to the tune. This tune from the fiddler's violin and the steps from the jigger's moccasins would become the most well-known Métis dance tune – it is unofficially called the national dance – and is seen at every Métis dance competition.

Others believe fiddle music and bagpipes are too far apart in pitch and key for that story to be true. Instead, the Red River Jig likely came from *Le Grande Gigue Simple*, a tune the French brought over with them. The complexity of the tune musically broken down can easily become the Red River Jig and since in those days no one had musical training, it's most likely that the voyageurs took the parts they could remember and played it in their own way – and thus it became what it is today.

At this festival, John wants to keep that traditional element intact and not let it evolve into something completely new. There are many other festivals that do that, although it is becoming increasingly more difficult to define what "traditional" means. The festival's website now states, in part, "we are not succeeding in having the contest be 'traditional - or - contemporary' and we are encountering problems separating the two. Disputes arose over traditional and non-traditional, fairness of judging, people dancing a traditional step but not dancing it 'traditionally' (eg); the formation of the step was correct, was either male or female - but - was danced with the feet raised way too high off the floor to be counted and judged as a traditional step." The debate continues.

John doesn't allow clickers and jiggers can wear whatever they like, keeping the festival atmosphere informal. Most jiggers throw on a Métis sash, but Yvonne, for example, always dressed in a full traditional dress with a beaded cummerbund and leggings when she competed.

"I honour the traditional," Yvonne tells me, "because I think it's a really important foundation for dancers to start off with, learning about their ancestors and honouring and respecting them," which includes the way she dresses. Her own company, Compaigni V'ni Dansi ("come and dance"), has similar dresses with handmade beadwork, a far cry from the trendy square dance outfits that most groups wear today.

"Today everything is flashy and the Métis adopted the square dance culture and created glittery outfits and are wearing clickers. A lot of performances nowadays are about spectacle, that's what's popular in the world today. It's rare to see traditional style. This generation is evolving, it's natural. But I'm grateful for the time I spent learning from elders like Maria Campbell, John Arcand, Kathleen Steinhauer and Gilbert Anderson, who made me who I am today." As a result of her dedication to the traditional, she won the 2011 Victor Martyn Lynch-Staunton award, which honours mid-career artists who are outstanding in seven different disciplines.

As an adjudicator, Yvonne sits at the judge's table out in the audience wearing a gorgeous, red long sleeved top, a black, colourfully beaded cummerbund, and a long, deep red skirt. She sits beside John and another judge, looking at me expectantly as I stand on the stage. This is the final of the Canadian Red River Jigging Championship and my last chance to show the judges all the fancy steps I have learned.

I nod a bit more confidently at the fiddler and can't help but beam at the audience and judges: I am thinking of a piece of Yvonne's advice after her last workshop. "If you forget which step to do, just keep smiling and do *something*. You won't get points for it, but just keep going."

I use that advice, too. After getting through about four steps, I let my mind wander. As Yvonne suggested, I turn a bit to face different parts of the audience and even spin around to do a few steps for the fiddlers, but get caught up in the enjoyment of the moment. The fancy part of the Red River Jig comes up and my feet fumble for a step to do. My smile grows wider as I keep jigging, but a mishmash of steps that definitely won't count roll through my feet. The fiddler saves me by switching back into the basic part of the tune, giving me time to come up with my next fancy step.

I get stuck about 10 steps in, unable to think of any more, but I finish with a final beat, grinning madly at the fun I'm having, and take my bow to the audience, judges and fiddlers. As I float happily down the stage stairs to the fading glory of the applause, I think back to Yvonne and her story of starting to compete: it was elders who told her to suck up her fears and get on stage, which is exactly what she told me to do two days ago.

"They said, 'You'd better get up there, get up there and do something.' So I said okay because when your elders tell you to do something, you don't say, 'No, I'm not going to do it.' You just get up there and you do it. So I went up and I won second place and I got the hook. I thought, 'Hey, well I must be pretty good, I must be not too bad, I must be doing something right if I got a second place trophy.' So I went back the next year and I learned some more steps and I learned more stuff, and I got first place. And then I went back again and I got first place, and I went back again and then Vicki asked me if I wanted to start teaching, and I was like, 'I just want to win that big overall trophy just once,' because I couldn't teach if I was competing."

So she went on to win the overall trophy the next year and, before she had even left the stage, John and Vicki asked her one last time: "You're going to teach, right?" And now she both teaches and judges. I have no ambition to ever teach Métis jigging, but I do think that a gentle push from someone you respect can be the best thing that happens, not only in dance, but in anything you love doing.

Yvonne, as well as studying contemporary dance in Winnipeg, Toronto and Vancouver, started her own companies when she settled in Vancouver, Compaigni V'ni Dansi for contemporary dance with Métis themes and the Louis Riel Métis Dancers for traditional Métis dance. She has since brought in Japanese choreographer Yukio Waguri for a piece on Louis Riel called *A Poet and Prophet*, has done a solo piece about the wife of Riel called *Marguerite*, *Gabriel's Crossing* about Métis chief Gabriel Dumont, a dance trilogy called *The Crossing* "that depicts the years of the Métis resistance from the hearts of the Métis people," and *Stories from St. Laurent*, based on oral traditions and dances gathered from Métis communities. Her traditional group performs at local events and festivals year round and has been partnering with musicians to host Louis Riel Day Celebrations across the Lower Mainland.

She also received a grant to create 10 Métis dance groups in B.C. through the First Peoples Heritage Language and Cultural Association. This took her to different communities in the province to help them establish small groups. "Not all of them survived, but some of them are still going." Other collaborations include well-known Métis artists and advocates like Maria Campbell, Marie Clements, Sandy Scofield and Jeff Harrison.

I remember asking Yvonne very seriously if she missed competing and how different it is to transition from getting up on stage with a championship on the line, to sharing her knowledge with others who now look up to her and, ultimately, decide whether they will win. I was sure she would lament the change and express how much she missed being a competitor. Instead, she just shrugged. "I just think it's fun… you can't take it too seriously." And that probably sums up the lively spirit of the Métis people.

Oh, and I did end up placing in the competition, fourth, and took home a $100 cheque. Along with the monetary prize, I was invited up onto the stage to receive it from John Arcand himself.

John's resolve to celebrate and focus on traditional dancing and music is not surprising, considering how hard the Métis population has fought to stand up for who they are. Canada, as we know it today – a multicultural patchwork, a constitutional monarchy, an enviable place to live – began its development as a country with the fur trade. European traders sailed overseas regularly after the Hudson's Bay Company, which controlled the fur trade for many centuries, received its royal charter in 1670 and then set up trading posts. Traders left their wives and children, if they were married, back in Europe.

But Canada has always been a difficult land to tame and the traders had to learn how to survive on vast stretches of wilderness that changed frequently. This they could only do with the help of the aboriginal people, those who had been living off the land since their arrival many thousands of years before.

Cultures inevitably clashed and fights ensued, but the one thing that has never changed is the need for companionship. The traders were in a foreign land and missed the company of women. Practically, as the times were back then, they also missed someone to do the cooking and cleaning and mending. On top of the things they were used to having done for them, they needed someone who knew how to take care of them from only the resources of the land. These things the First Nations women had learned from their mothers and grandmothers since they were little girls.

When European men and First Nations women began getting married (sometimes by choice, but other times women were forced to marry), the French voyageurs in Quebec romantically called those who would become the Métis people ("mixed" in French), *les enfants d'amour* ("children of love") because "both arms were open to each other." So open, in fact, that the historically correct answer, say some, to the question, When did the Métis people originate, is: nine months after the first white man set foot in Canada.

Métis is a more recent name for the children of the union between First Nations and Europeans. Half of each culture, this new generation, and their children's children, are of mixed backgrounds, taking traditions and beliefs from each of their parents. Historically they were called Half Breeds, not as a name used behind closed doors or whispered derogatorily behind their backs (although it was definitely used derogatorily), but as their everyday title, even used on official documents.

They were considered "nothings," half "Indian" and half "white" but rejected by both cultures. They were thought to be inferior to each "real" culture. This would play a huge role when land claim negotiations started, and it still does, because the Métis' rights were never defined. If they were considered "Indians," they were entitled to a certain amount of land, free education for their children and could live on reserves subsidized by the government; if they identified as Métis, they didn't receive those things, but were instead offered scrip, either land scrip or money scrip, as the law tried to simplify a very complex situation.

The waters were murky and the government probably hoped that the Métis would eventually assimilate into either one of their cultures and would not have to be dealt with again. Scrip forced the Métis to either identify as "Indian" or renounce their "Indian" status, which would have consequences for future generations of their family, especially since the laws of scrip changed frequently, as did provincial and federal policies. Those who accepted either a piece of land or money (or took the land and then sold it to a broker who feasted on their need for instant cash) relinquished their aboriginal title and lived as "whites." Others went onto Indian Reserves and lived as "Indians."

As with any children of mixed heritage, they often look more like one parent than the other, some passing quite easily as First Nations and others from European descent, so most children assimilated into the most obvious culture while hiding their mixed heritage. Sometimes families wanted this for their children, so parents and grandparents would only speak one language at home, usually English, and hide their mixed identity. Instead of being half of each culture, then, most chose one to be identified with.

Even as the Métis population grew inevitably larger, they dealt with the same prejudices as before, never really fitting in with either the First Nations or newly settled European communities. As they helped carve the way of the fur traders' voyage west, the area of the Red River

Valley (presently Winnipeg) became the heart of the Métis people, the only place where their large numbers allowed them to not have to choose between cultures, where they could just be themselves.

By the first half of the 19th century, the Métis were forming their own identity in this isolated area, not as two halves but as one whole of their own. In 1816, they declared themselves a new nation with a flag featuring the infinity symbol. In 1870, they were a major factor in the forming of the province of Manitoba. But tensions grew taut and when the Dominion of Canada and the Hudson's Bay Company arranged for the land that included the Red River Valley (then called Rupert's Land) to be transferred without their consultation, they formed their own provisional government to fight for their rights. This eventually led to the historic 1885 Resistance or Northwest Rebellion, led by the most famous Métis man of all, Louis Riel.

They fought for their land rights, they fought for their own social structure and, most importantly, they fought for their autonomy. Constantly thought of as inferior, the Métis showed what they could become if they banded together.

Unfortunately for them, the battle was lost in Batoche and led a lot of the population to move farther west to Saskatchewan, or south to Dakota and Montana. Louis Riel was eventually hanged for treason and the Métis had to continue to fight for their autonomy, which they still do today to a lesser degree. The Métis were officially recognized in the 1982 Constitutional Act as an aboriginal group next to First Nations and Inuit, but their rights were not defined.

With the forming of their own separate culture and a growing passion to be proud of their heritage, the Métis, known for their lively spirit and propensity for having a good time, have always been enthusiastic dancers. In fact, the joke goes that if you want to drive a Métis person crazy, you nail his shoes to the ground and put on Andy De Jarlis (a phenomenal traditional Métis fiddler).

The most well-known of the Métis dances is the Red River Jig, which spread in the late 1700s until it was known "from James Bay to Alaska," as *The Dances of the Métis* video produced by the Métis Resource Centre in Winnipeg puts it. It is still considered the national dance. Some historians believe that the Red River Jig is "one of the few truly Canadian dance forms," as it was born from the First Nations and Europeans, the population of which Canada was founded with in 1867 – the first Canadians.

To keep warm on cold Canadian nights and to keep entertained all year round, the Métis would have jigging competitions to see who could do the most fancy steps to the Red River Jig tune. Dancers would mix what they had learned from the First Nations dances of their mothers and the reels from their fathers, doing intricate footwork to an upbeat fiddle tempo, adding some competitive fun, and dancing all night. This was *their* dance.

Back then, the Red River Jig was more of an elimination dance, where challengers would try to outdo each other by the number of steps they could pull off in their repertoire. They would be surrounded by cheering traders in a community hall, if they had one, candlelight flickering as their footwork eluded the shadows; they could be in a house where the furniture had been removed so they had room to do something more important than sitting around on chairs: dancing and playing music.

Often the groups would gather by 8:00 p.m. and not disperse until 5:00 a.m. the next morning. Some accounts say they danced for days, or until their liquor, food and energy had been jigged out of them.

Other accounts say the Red River Jig was done by two people, either two men or a man and a woman, who danced together or challenged other couples to compete against them. This was their time to be recognized as individual dancers, unlike the group dances so popular back then, and they were rewarded with community respect and probably some whiskey.

John Arcand keeps that spirit alive at his fiddle festival by formalizing it a little bit. Most people don't spend their nights out on the land looking for entertainment and a way to keep warm anymore – they're inside a house in a community or a city with their computers and TVs fired up, not with candlelight, but from the power from their local electricity company.

On John and Vicki's property, contestants are split up into age groups and between male and female. After qualifying by showing they know the steps in the first round, the finalists then go up on stage to dance as many steps as they can remember. Judges tally up how many they completed (not counting steps that are off rhythm or not precise enough, or, for the traditional category, steps that are considered contemporary – ie. not low to the ground, with the legs reaching up above the ankles or shaking out to the side). Often, there are clear first, second, third and fourth place winners, each receiving a cheque from the festival, but other times the second place dancer feels he or she can do better than the person who came in first place and challenges him or her to a dance off.

This happened in the adult men's category the year I was there. Two men had competed hard in the finals and the second place man decided that he could outdo the first place dancer. They both took to the stage together in a dancing dual. In previous years, there used to be duet competitions, in honour of the accounts that said that the Red River Jig was done in pairs, but this was taken out to make room for the elder's category, an important change that now allows elders who are still dancing to compete with those their own age.

With the two dancers on stage, the first place dancer acts as the leader, doing a fancy step that the challenger has to pick up while the tune keeps playing. Step by step the first place dancer tries some of his most complex steps to throw his competitor off; the challenger tries to keep up by repeating every step he sees. If the first place dancer runs out of steps but his competitor can come up with one more, not already used, then the challenger becomes the first place winner, knocking the original winner into second place.

While steadfastly concentrating on the other's feet – one was wearing beige moccasins and the other black dress shoes, both wearing t-shirts and jeans – the dancers faced each other and jigged step after step in a circular shape. In keeping with tradition, the basic steps were jigged in a travelling circle, while the fancy steps were danced facing each other on the spot. Both had a fluid quality that seemed to keep their knees bouncing as if effortless, and although they were dancing for first place, they never showed signs of tension in their upper bodies as they thought of the next step. Even as the minutes ticked by, they still looked like they were dancing on air, even laughing a bit at new steps and as the crowd cheered.

The challenger ended up fumbling a step, so the first place jigger did end up in first place after all. It was a good, old fashioned duel and left the audience buzzing. Too bad there was no whisky.

Sarah Quick, who is doing her doctoral research at Indiana University on Métis identity, performance and heritage, found in her research that rules used to be a tad bit different. She writers in her essay, *The Social Poetics of the Red River Jig in Alberta and Beyond: Meaningful Heritage and Emerging Performance*, "An example is the story of how challenges in the past were determined by jiggers having to dance with a shot of whisky placed on a saucer on top of these jiggers' heads: the winner was decided based on who spilled the least amount of whisky." Elders also say that it was a saucer and wine glass placed on the top of the dancer's heads, the winner being the one with the most wine left at the end.

Times change, cultures change, dances change, but every adaptation is influenced by something before it. In the Métis culture, that is low-to-the-ground, intricate footwork and tight steps; from there, dancers have created contemporary steps that lift the legs above the ankles when they used to stay grounded, or shake the legs out to the side when they used to just tap their toe out; some performing dancers wear clickers and stomp loudly; and other cultures are influencing new steps as dance videos from all over the world can be seen on websites like YouTube. Most importantly, though, is keeping this evidence of culture from the days of life on the Red River alive, a crucial reminder of survival.

Square dancing is just as popular as jigging, especially because more people can take part. Jigging still remains the base of the dances, though, as it is done even during many of the travelling steps and in between square sets. These were directly passed on from Europe, with dances like the Reel of Eight, Seven Steps, Drops of Brandy (*danse de crochet*), the Duck Dance, the Waltz Quadrille and, of course, the Red River Jig, being the most popular. But they went far beyond just learning the steps.

As Maria Campbell, a renowned Métis writer and historian, says in the documentary, *How the Fiddle Flows*: "Home was those stories and that music… Those step dances were a challenging dance; they were almost a flirting dance. For a young girl dancing, you're hoping that some guy is going to notice you. But your grandmother had taught you that you had to be all covered up and you had to be really subtle about everything, so you learned how to do all those things just by the way you moved your skirt or the kind of steps you took."

Then the language used by the square dance callers began mixing, with English and French often being used in the same sentence: *à la main gauche* (to your left hand) became *à la main* left, which is still used today when callers say, "allemande left."

Although jigging always had a competitive edge to it, square dancing went from a whole community jumping into different sets to formal competitions like the one at Back to Batoche Days in Saskatchewan, a large annual celebration honouring Métis culture and historical figures. Square dance culture has become exceedingly popular and groups from all over the world compete by being more and more spectacular. Some groups now love stomping their feet and have a blast dressed in modern outfits, even competing in the newly created Métis' Got Talent category.

There isn't any acrobatic moves or high-flying tricks in square dancing, and some dances only allude to the traditional sets they are based on. Now, dancers can be seen wearing shiny outfits made of satin, with frills along the necklines and at the bottom of skirts; bright ruffles underneath skirts keeps them bouncy and full; and some wear clickers on their feet to articulate the sound of their footwork. Judges evaluate groups based on their changes, or "break downs," at varying speeds. And whereas there would almost always be a caller at a Métis dance, that is also missing from most dances these days.

Instead of following in their elders' footsteps, though, the younger dancers are creating new ways to make Métis dancing relevant to them by infusing hip hop- and pow wow-influenced moves into the mix; comedians are jigging while telling their jokes and plays are incorporating the Red River Jig in their storylines.

This is a completely different atmosphere than at the John Arcand Fiddle Fest, where there isn't a square dance competition, just fiddling and the Red River Jig competitions. Actually, the year I went was the first time there was prize money for contemporary dancers at all. As the rules stated then: "As things evolve and change, we see a development of many more people dancing the Red River jig, in what for lack of a better term, John is calling Contemporary or Modern Style, and we feel we need to support those efforts as well, but also feel it's necessary to separate the two in order to continue our goal of preserving the traditional style."

There are no square dancing outfits, and no clickers allowed, and jiggers compete in their jeans, t-shirts and running shoes, often with a colourful Métis sash draped over their shoulder or around their waist. It is all just for casual fun, like it always has been.

I remember Yvonne telling me about her times competing at the festival and what stood out the most for her wasn't the trophies or the outcome, it was the excitement of challenging herself to know as many steps as she could and the joy that jigging brought her.

"I was just so happy to be up there and dancing. It was such a good vibe," she says without hesitation.

I felt the same way. After getting on a stage again and being given a challenge – that of the tricky Red River Jig – I remembered all those times I had danced in front of audiences growing up and the feeling of energy that would surge through my blood long after I had stopped dancing. Or maybe a dancers' body never does stop dancing. A Métis person's jigs always buzzes around in their veins, a ballerina's *jetés* always pumps through her legs and the chance to move with music, to compete and to perform is the outlet of what cannot be held inside.

The Métis people were considered worth half as human beings, dismissed as never belonging to one culture, doomed to be forgotten as they lost themselves in another's traditions. But that didn't happen. That *something* inside of them was always dancing and finally found an outlet: a new culture that gave them that same elation that competing and performing fosters, an outlet where there was pride instead of shame at where they came from and what they could become. And although they are still fighting for everyone to recognize that *something*, they now know what it is and can vow together to not let it be taken away.

Although some of the modern changes that have been added to Métis dancing (and I'm sure the same is true for fiddling) will make some elders cringe, the fact that young people are involved in the traditions and care enough to make their own adaptations and to make the old work for them in the now, is the best way forward. They are the ones who will keep the traditions from being locked away as just memories. As long as they always remember where the original steps came from – and festivals like John and Vicki Arcand's remain true to that heritage – they can keep them alive injected with their own creativity.

"You can't just live a traditional life anymore," Yvonne tells me over a cup of tea at her Vancouver apartment, "and it's not good just to live in the contemporary world, either. You need to embrace both."

What Vicki and John are doing on their acreage is making sure that no one forgets where these dances started. And sometimes, doesn't it just feel *right* to do things the way they used to be done?

There is square dancing at the John Arcand Fiddle Fest, but it doesn't come in the form of a competition; rather, as an old time dance on both the Friday and Saturday nights. Here the chairs are pushed aside once more to open the wooden stage up as a dance floor.

By the time I arrive on Saturday night, the sun has gone down but has left behind its warmth long enough for us to stir up our own heat. It is the last night I will be at Windy Acres and the last night of the festival for this year. I arrive to the fiddlers already playing a tune and the first dancers making their way around the makeshift stage two by two, their friends and family occupying the surrounding chairs, tapping their feet to the music. I only know the people I have chatted with throughout the weekend, a few of whom I see already dancing, yet I feel as though I have arrived at a friend's party.

Before I have even put my purse down on a chair, an old timer whom I recognize from the jigging competition pulls me up onto the dance floor with a tireless (or is it timeless?) grin. "You weren't thinkin' of sittin' down now were ya?" he laughs.

We make our way to the opposite side of the floor and a new tune starts. I can tell by the collective intake of breath, the quick smiles and the nod to their partners that everyone recognizes it. My partner looks me in the eye, puts his right hand around my waist, takes my left hand in his and says, "Let's go!"

I have no idea where we're going, but I'm happy to follow along. We start waltzing, zigzagging through other couples, spinning around newcomers, laughing as we meet the same faces; the tune is fast, faster than any I've ever waltzed to before, and has what I'd call a Métis kick to it, that upbeat zing that keeps you quite literally on your toes.

The summer air isn't stuffy or hot, but I can already feel the moisture trying to cool my skin after the first tune. The next elicits another familiar whoop from the crowd and, knowing there is no question that we will keep going, my partner this time stands beside me and we link hands across the front – our left hands together and our right hands together – and move forward with the group in a clockwise direction.

Different couples are doing different footwork, but I follow my partner with a travelling jig step similar to what I learned in the first Red River Jig workshop. I soon abandon looking down at his feet as I notice I am missing all the action. Yes, we are all doing similar yet different steps, but the fun part is not in the footwork, it is in the interaction: the eye contact and winks as I pass one couple and the open-mouthed laugh as I pass another. Our collective breathing infuses the air with a sort of drug-like glint that spreads from smile to smile like an infectious bug that everyone wants to catch.

My partner can handle no more and he finally heads to a chair to sit down, but the bug has obviously infected those watching from the sidelines as the dance floor is filled to capacity again and I find myself moving with two women I met earlier in the day. We all recognize each other at the same time and then fall into step without a word of instruction, just a quick scan of what each other is doing with their feet.

Off we go flitting around the dance floor like we have known each other our whole lives, comfortable spending the night with our arms around each other and other newly-made friends. I am laughing and consistently doing the wrong steps, breathing in and out with the untainted rhythm of a child. This is an old time dance, Métis style.

CANADA

ALBERTA

SASKATCHEWAN

Jasper

Saskatoon

USA

7 Saskatchewan and Alberta: Let's Dance Ukrainian Style

The line up twists around the lobby twice when I arrive at TCU Place in Saskatoon, the city's arts and convention centre. My assumption before getting here was that this festival was a minor annual event for the small Ukrainian community in the city; I expected homemade banners and loonie store balloons. Yet, either every family in Saskatoon is here or the Ukrainian community is larger than I anticipated, all dressed up and ready to party.

The line starts to move down the stairs and into the huge lower hall as we all shuffle forward amid a buzz of chatter. There are young children dressed in tiny suit jackets and flowery dresses; teenagers obey the "no blue denim" rule and appear glad to be able to pull out their fancy eveningwear (one 15-year old girl would later tell me, "I seriously wait for this festival every year"); parents and grandparents are in their weekend best; and I have dusted off a formal burgundy dress that has been hanging forlornly in my closest for about five years.

As I reach the door and hand over my ticket, the volunteer smiles and enthuses, "Welcome to the Vesna Festival!" I step inside and into another world underneath the prairie streets.

The first order of business is to grab a bite to eat. It's Friday night around dinnertime and my stomach is doing a hunger dance. I had been told that the homemade food here would be just as important as the dancing, so I wander over to the long buffet-style tables on one side of the hall, where a line up has already been formed. Dish after dish of Ukrainian food lines the tables. I dump *varenyky* (perogies), *holubtsi* (cabbage rolls) and *borscht* (beetroot soup) on my plate, also eyeing the *kovbasa* (sausage) and chicken *kyiv* (chicken rolled up with herbs, breaded and then fried or baked). For dessert there is Café Kyiv, an area with a collection of homemade cakes, tortes, sweets, specialty coffees and tea.

I scan the crowd and find an empty seat at the end of a long table facing the stage and crisscross through the gaggle of children running around in folk costumes. Their parents look relaxed and ready to let loose and their grandparents sit at tables proudly as the next generation upholds a culture they brought with them to Canada so many years ago.

A father whom I had chatted with in the first line up comes over to me as I am digging into a perogy. "Are you ready?" he smiles. "This is like one big Ukrainian wedding, but without the bride and groom!"

Vesna means spring and a time the Slavs would use to usher in the new year that was coming. They celebrated by dancing and singing traditional ritualistic songs called *vesnyanky,* although in the western regions they were also known as *hahilky, hayivky, yahilky* and *rohulky.* This *vesna* festival in Saskatoon takes place every May to celebrate the spring season. Although many of the families here are supporting children who are dancing, there are many others who make an effort to be here every year to support the festival and to stay connected with the community.

Ukrainian dance was completely unfamiliar to me before I came to the Vesna Festival, save for the similar Russian splits and jumps (and the Russian hat dance) I had seen men perform in movies. I imagined colourful blouses and folksy steps, but was otherwise in the dark.

After watching the first dance, I am reminded that dancing has a way of surpassing many barriers, no matter where it comes from or what steps are used: dancers can tell whole stories with their bodies, using a gesture here or a flick of a leg there. The dances are mostly based on folk stories and traditional songs, but no Ukrainian words are needed. Specific costumes chosen from a particular region, colours that represent a certain area and music that provides the plot all tell the choreographer where to go with his or her movements.

Serhij Koroliuk, the Artistic Director of the Pavlychenko Folklorique Ensemble (who performs at the festival), says exactly that. "To me it doesn't matter which language the dancers speak, their nationality or what ground they come from. I just want them to speak the language of Ukrainian dance. It is the language I use to talk with the audience. My definition of dance is movement is a living expression of the soul… If you look at the different nations and nationalities, the dance actually talks; it can tell about a nation's character."

I put that to the test when, in between performances, the band plays and the dance floor opens up to the audience. I get swept up in the crowd a few times, getting lost among the pink faces and mix of dresses, suits and traditional folk costumes; sweaty people are joining hands and doing their own version of Ukrainian steps, or fooling around and adding cheesy 80s moves or other snippets from modern culture. This type of atmosphere is closer to what Ukrainian dance is based on, which is folk dancing, where people are dancing for themselves, not for an audience. The biggest difference is that I'm not sure if the *babas* recognize some of these pop-inspired steps…

When the band stops playing, we all go back to our tables (well, I join the children sitting on the floor at the front) and wait for another performance. What I see on the stage differs greatly from the steps rural folks used to do in Ukraine, of course. Pavlo Virsky is seen as one of the first choreographers in Ukraine to take traditional dances and share them with an audience (this idea was based on the work of Vasyl Verkhovynets). As a professionally trained choreographer who specialized in ballet, Virsky wanted to apply the rules of composition that he used for his own choreography and insert them into Ukrainian folk dances. His lead has been followed by many contemporary choreographers and is what we see now when a Ukrainian dance group performs.

As Serhij explains to me, "Basically, when you're witnessing what happened to Irish dance with Riverdance and the Lord of the Dance, the same thing happened here except Ukrainians did it back in the 50s and 60s. Pavlo Virsky conceived of a way to merge folk and classical dance. He applied traditional rules of dramatic composition, development of plot, climax, conclusion, like writing a story or screenplay. Different dances, different characters, different costumes, basically folk-like opera, but folk dance. It's well organized, well composed and polished and brought to the stage. What Riverdance did with Irish dance, modernizing it, but keeping the roots. So that's what the idea was."

Serhij's purpose in directing his company is to not just replicate what was done centuries ago. "We're not just trying to preserve Ukrainian culture, but also to develop it, with respect to all those pioneers. A museum contains artefacts that don't exist anymore, you just go and see how it was. We are trying to show that Ukrainian staged dance has roots from the old country but that it's a living, evolving thing."

In his own choreography, Serhij takes traditional folk formations and finds ways to adapt them for the audience, in effect, changing it from social dancing to performance dancing. What was once a circle becomes a semi-circle, opening up to the crowd, and lines are introduced where all dancers face towards the viewers. This adaptation allows the choreographer to share stories with an audience that might be seeing Ukrainian dance for the first time.

"Make it as authentic as possible," continues Serhij. "When you're doing choreography, you have to follow the rules of the stage because, when you do a social dance in a circle, everybody's dancing, so there's no distinction between participants or observers. On the stage, dancers perform for the audience. Playing by these rules, you have to open the circle to show the audience what's going on. People in the audience who are not participating want to see. So in choreography, that circle opens into a semi-circle, turns into lines, etc… These are some of the tricks that I always have to consider when telling a story on stage."

If dance tells the stories of a country, then the *hopak* represents the celebratory spirits of the independent Ukrainian people. It is often referred to as the National Dance of Ukraine. The word *hopak* translates into jump or hop, an apt description of the movements. The Cossacks are reported in historical accounts as coming into their own in the early 15th century. Many serfs and peasants fled their villages after being fed up with feudal exploitation and an army of people called the Cossacks ("free people") were considered their saviours with their wild, high energy spirit.

By the 16th century, they had developed the *hopak* as a social dance to be done after a victorious battle, mainly in central Ukraine around the Dnipro River. The male mercenaries, after proving their manliness on the battlefield, would replicate it by acting out the fight that had just taken place, improvising acrobatic jumps and leaps, and demonstrating their speed and heroism with the challenging steps they could do.

In the mid 1600s, the Cossacks led a rebellion in Ukraine against the Polish-Lithuanian Commonwealth known as the Khmelnytsky Uprising or Rebellion. As other classes joined them in the fight, they succeeded in gaining independence from Polish rule. The Cossacks were seen as wild, gallant warriors who spread their songs and dances to the villages with unleashed creativity.

As news spread of their victories, villagers would celebrate by dancing in the Cossack way to show their support. Both men and women joined in, although the men still retained the leading role, and elements that braided in more traditional village dances added formations and pairs dancing together to the festivities. The music would be played to match the dancer's energy and varied tempos, changing melodies and speed. The *hopak* is still one of the most popular Ukrainian dances today, although stylized through many years of adaptations.

In western Ukraine, the Hutsul people who live in the Carpathian Mountains developed their own style of dancing that represented their regional traditions. One of these dances was the *arkan* (meaning lasso), which was danced around a fire. The men would surround it and try to keep the circle intact while repeating steps. Putting their hands on each other's shoulders, the men would listen for the caller to shout out the next step, which would then be repeated. The movements would progress faster and the tempo would increase, the men adjusting their steps each time the caller would yell, all the while not breaking the circle. It was almost like a moving meditation.

"It's like what hockey players do before they go on the ice, right?" Serhij asks me rhetorically. "Hands on shoulders, 'Let's do this, guys.'"

Serhij has taken this traditional dance and moved it into the modern arena. The piece I saw at the Vesna Festival had eight men dressed in various costumes, some in white peasant shirts with thick black belts and others with dark coats overtop of maroon pants. They were doing similar steps that the pagan men would have done: tight, fast, strong movements.

"That's what the Ukrainian Highlanders did with this dance. My idea was to keep the main steps of this dance and these steps should be executed a certain way. I try to keep the authentic steps but I develop them to a different vision of the dance."

It was a variation of the *arkan* and Serhij used a rope to connect the male and female dancers around the waist. Eventually they opened up the circle to interact more with the audience and used some solo time to show off their unique skills.

"So, in this particular arkan I broke with tradition," he explains. "At the beginning of my version of this dance, there was a whole circle to establish the *arkan's* authentic origin and then the circle breaks to a semi-circle so the audience can see what's going on."

Serhij then took the "lasso" and used it as a large skipping rope. And then the fun really began in *hopak*-like style. Each of the dancers took to the spotlight: two people stood on either side of the long rope and swung it in a circle, just like on the school playground. One at a time, a dancer would step in and perform their stunt to the noisy crowd. In this way, they were "keeping the circle" by not stopping the rope. If anyone took a misstep or made a mistake, they would have broken the circle and the dance would have been over.

"The steps are still from the authentic *arkan* or lasso," Serhij continues with his contagious enthusiasm, "not just a meditation or togetherness, but fun and challenging… They now have to show their skill by performing steps and they can't mess up!"

His adaptations are obviously an audience favourite. During the show, family members are yelling out their brother, sister, boyfriend, girlfriend, son or daughter's name as he or she takes centre stage to perform a trick; the crowd is hollering at the top of their lungs with each new dancer. Whether it's the steady stream of alcohol the adults are putting away or the sheer passion of the crowd, the place is especially crazy during this dance.

Interpretations like this are one reason why Serhij loves being in Canada so much. He can do things here that might not be accepted with the same gusto as back home. He tells me about one student of his in particular that makes me smile. It's a young girl who wanted to do the more athletic dances that the boys were practising, so Serhij encouraged her, and other girls, to try them.

"The girls can kick butt, they can do fun stuff, they want a challenge. That's something that is created in Canada; I wouldn't probably do this in Ukraine. At the end of the piece [being performed, the girls] take their hats off and their hair is down and you can see [they're not boys]. They're doing split jumps, flips and all the funky stuff, athletic, fighting with swords, showing their skills, that usually guys do."

When Ukrainian immigrants began coming to Canada in 1891, Pam Trischuk, at the Ukrainian Cultural Heritage Village just outside of Edmonton, tells me that they were too busy working the land in order to survive to put much energy into their dance traditions. Instead of the less than five acres of land they probably would have had in Ukraine, the Canadian government attracted them with an offer of 160 acres for $10. There was much work to be done here and little time for social gatherings.

Dance was rarely seen until the 1920s, when farmers began seeing success from their crops and settlements could build community halls for socializing. This is when Ukrainian dance was really born in Canada and the people haven't stopped dancing since. It all comes back to letting dance be the language for a culture's character, even through modern adaptations.

Even though Ukrainian dance in Canada still comes from Ukraine, it's danced here through a Canadian filter. In Serhij's opinion, "It is second hand from Ukraine because of its origin. Ukrainian pioneers brought it over as a part of their folk culture, the village version, so to say. The first Ukrainian dance choreographer, Vasyl Avramenko, known as the father of Ukrainian dance in Canada, came from Ukraine, and many of our present day Ukrainian-Canadian choreographers are either originally from Ukraine, or have studied this genre in Ukraine or from Ukrainian instructors in Canada.

"So, the influence of the 'Ukrainian style' of dancing is very pronounced. Many Canadian born dancers can Ukrainian dance with 'no accent,' just as many choreographers and instructors speak English with a Ukrainian accent or can easily fake it since they've been to Ukraine so many times or grew up in Canada as 'Ukies.'

"Despite the 'second hand' expression, I see that Ukrainian dance in Canada is not just a copy of its master version from the old country. This genre is growing and developing in Canada, taking different angles, bringing fresh ideas and reflecting the culture and mentality of Canadian society. Having said that, I am not trying to separate Ukrainian dance into two different kinds, it's all connected. But the genre becomes more independent and unique. It represents not only Ukrainian, but Canadian culture. I guess it's like a different dialect of the same language."

Serhij created a piece called Canadian Kaleidoscope that his group performs as part of their repertoire. "It's a 20-minute piece with all performing cast hidden under a big huge Canadian flag, surrounded by flags from different countries. They pull the flag out and there are numerous people in different quadrants coming out, starting from Native dance, Scottish, Irish, French, Filipino, German, Ukrainian, and then at the very end they all sing Oh Canada. It's not just multi-region, it's multi-genre… I wouldn't create this in Ukraine. It's a very Canadian mentality."

Interestingly, when his group toured through Ukraine in 2003, they were well-received. "When the Canadian anthem was playing, we had a standing ovation from the audience in each city. I think we did six cities… They didn't say our dances were unlike theirs, they recognized the dance and they were pleased to see Canadians who know Ukrainian dance keep and respect traditions. But for numbers like kaleidoscope, they said, 'Yeah, this is a different twist.' They were very proud of how Canadians present the culture from the old country… It was very touching."

***

Not finished with my newfound interest in Ukrainian dancing, I decide to drag my Ukrainian friend Anastasia to Jasper the next January for some more fun. Anastasia had been a Ukrainian dancer and instructor in Edmonton for almost 30 years and she hadn't been to Malanka (Ukrainian New Years) in a long time.

We pack our bags and make the road trip to the Fairmont Jasper Park Lodge, which has been putting on this Malanka celebration since its inception in 1997. The front desk staff are into the spirit, the women wearing *sorochka* (folk blouses) and the men wearing *sharovary* (the wide Cossack pants); a giant Christmas tree fills out the lobby and a Ukrainian tone takes over the entire hotel. Just like at the Vesna Festival, children, teenagers, parents and grandparents mingle together in formalwear, the young girls often stealing away to the washroom to giggle and primp in front of the mirrors.

Malanka at the Jasper Park Lodge is meant to cover all of the Ukrainian holiday traditions in one weekend, including St. Nicholas Day, Christmas Eve, New Years Eve, and the Feast of Jordan or Theophany. Many families make it a plan to be here every year, gathering together instead of celebrating in their separate homes and cities. It's typically Ukrainian, I'm told.

Tonight is the warm up, a gentle Friday night prelude to ease us into the program. By 8:30 p.m., the ballroom is heaving with folk music, smiling dancers and clapping audience members cheering on their performing friends and family.

The revelry really begins on Saturday night. I sit with Anastasia at a round table among many other round tables getting a lesson on which dishes everyone thinks will be served. Traditionally, 12 dishes are cooked for Christmas Eve supper to represent the 12 apostles. This is the end of the Fast of St. Philip and the beginning of the Christmas season. But this isn't going to be a strictly traditional meal, as it's actually billed as a Malanka dinner. A gentleman across the table from me says that the Fairmont usually prepares a mostly Ukrainian meal but peppers it with a few other dishes for those who want non-traditional options.

As everyone debates what constitutes traditional and what is just an add-on, I look up to my right and notice the bishop and two sisters in habits walking over to our table, here this weekend to perform the Sunday services and join in on the festivities. They sit down beside me, the bishop introducing himself first. A few at the table already know him from church and the rest of us introduce ourselves politely.

The sisters are here temporarily from Ukraine and have joined the bishop in Edmonton for a few months. They speak fairly good English but are quite shy and sit quietly for most of the evening talking between themselves. The bishop kicks things off with an offer to buy the table a bottle of wine, "to get it flowing," he says with a wink. The sisters timidly but happily partake in a few glasses and we take care of the rest.

The star of the evening performances is the Vohon Ukrainian Dance Ensemble, a group of about 40 dancers from Edmonton who mix traditional dancing with a hint of contemporary styles. Tammy Komarnisky Myskiw, an ex-dancer and now instructor with Vohon, explains that other dance forms are used now, not only for training, but in performance.

"We all take ballet, we all use that as a foundation now for all the groups and character technique and all of that," she tells me over a cocktail and a glass of wine at the lodge. "I think for our group, we definitely do incorporate the jazz, the modern, the ballet. That's probably the three main dance styles that we try to infuse... I danced for 30 years and probably in the first three or four years that I started dancing, ballet was already introduced as a sort of a foundation for dancing."

The dancers wear bright, colourful costumes with great pride. I remember Anastasia describing the costumes from the Bukovyna region: They have "beautiful colours, the blouses would always be these bold pinks and purples and reds, and there would always be these beautiful flowers and very pronounced embroidery. It wouldn't be just simple red and black central Ukrainian embroidery just in a band on the arm, these would go all the way down the arm. It was just so rich in colour and breadth of embroidery."

Authentic costumes add to the conversation that dancing starts. For Tammy, "a performance is a communication between the audience and the performers. People might not think that way, but it is. We're having a conversation: I'm dancing, you're watching. There's a connection there and it can be very powerful for the dancer on stage, as well as the person in the audience. And so I think folk dance is very important and it's important on many levels. Folk dance in its truest essence is important for the person because they feel part of that group, or that community, or that moment in time and how they fit into it.

"It's like an onion: there are many levels to it and maybe for different dancers the layers of the onion might be a little bit different... And I love social dance; it's a connection to who I am, the community and my heritage."

Ukrainian dance tells the stories of its history, societal issues and traditional values, which is what Vohon strives to do in its performances.

"Vohon prides itself on its use of storyline in a show. We have always maintained that essential in creating an artistic medium for people to relate to because people can relate to dance, and there's an emotion in dance. Every movement we do is part of an action and reaction. So we actually do a two hour storyline when we dance, so all of our dancers are weaved into a story. For today's modern audience, because we attract not just Ukrainian audiences but audiences from abroad, especially when we tour internationally, which we do every two years, people can relate. They think, 'Oh, wow, Ukrainian dance is so cool because of all the tricks and all of that,' but we have a story so people can relate to the story, too.

"For example, we did The King's Court when we went to Asia. It was about a king who was unhappy with his life. He had everything, right, he's the king, and in all the dances, everybody tried to make him happy, and it didn't work. What he found out at the end of the storyline was that his love for his wife and family were what made him happy. And so he went through this sort of transformation and we weaved the story through dance…

"When we performed in Thailand, they have a king and queen, and we did The King's Court and so when we performed – it was an outdoors venue and people just sat on the grass and they watched the show – and afterwards, they thought we were celebrities and they connected to this because they have a king… I got this bracelet because I was the queen during the show, beautiful silver. A young girl came up to us, took pictures with us, and she's like, 'No, no, no, here have this.' Obviously we spoke to them in some way. We don't have the language to communicate, but we touched them on some level. And that's very powerful."

The narrative Vohon creates doesn't stop when the dancers leave the stage. The conversation continues even when the music has stopped, whether it is feedback from first time audience members or people like

Anastasia sharing with me the memories that are brought back when she sees a performance. To some, dance itself becomes its own language and replaces words.

"When we danced in Australia," Tammy continues, "some people said, 'Well, you're not speaking Ukrainian,' to some of our dancers, so 'you can't be Ukrainian.' Because for them, the [spoken] language is what makes us Ukrainian. [But] for many of the dancers, dance is the medium that portrays who they are as Ukrainian."

"One of my dance students this year, she's going to a junior high that has a bilingual Polish part and just a regular program [girl's school]. She made a connection with one of the boys in the Polish program – he's a Polish dancer – and she's like, 'Oh, I want to see what you do' because that was their link into each other's culture, which was very cool. So he came to see her at the Christmas concert and she's going to go watch him and it's interesting how now we can share on a level. If we use language as our connector, we couldn't, because we'd be speaking totally different languages. But dance is becoming that medium that connects a province, which I think is very cool and very interesting.

"I know that when we performed in Adelaide at a dance festival (I think it was a children's festival, but none of us were children at the time, we were all adults), there were people there from around the world. We could not communicate because they were speaking, you know, there was a Jordan group and then there was a Chinese group. How did we communicate? We watched each others' dancing. And then, you know, we gave thumbs up, high fives and spoke in smiles. We bought their CD, this one group, and we tried to mimic their dancing because we couldn't do it. That's the group from Jordan.

"So we were sharing dance moves and it was very interesting that dynamic that the world is so large and we all have such diverse cultural backgrounds, but we could connect on a level. And dance was that level because it wasn't verbal, so language was not a barrier. We were just in awe to see that dance and vice versa… In a world perspective, there is so much that we can learn from each other just through dance."

The way people dance around the world has everything to do with the way societies behave, how communities have survived over history, the beliefs that define their culture and the freedom they have lost or found along the way. Within that, each region or village has their own unique way of doing things. In Ukraine, for example, their national struggles are similar, but their regional lifestyles vary widely. So, too, do their dances.

When a dance is representing the Hutsul region in the Carpathian Mountains, dancers wear vests, wool socks and leather elf-like shoes; their steps are very perpendicular because there isn't much level room on the mountains to do large, sweeping steps sideways, whereas, on the plains, where the space is wide open and warmer, steps can spread out and be expansive.

This is the same in Canada, too. Although most choreography still stays true to the Ukrainian regional make up of the dance, it has been Canadian-ized. When part of a population immigrates to a new country, the way the lifestyle of the community changes is reflected in the steps they choose to dance together; the rhythm of a society in everyday life is mirrored in the way they dance.

The oldest form of Ukrainian folk art is the ritual dance, minute components of which still exist today. These dances revolved around welcoming in each new season and included three types: agricultural work (the process of harvesting a crop, for example), social-familial relationships and their respect for nature.

Combined with poetry and music, these dances were rituals that corresponded to the yearly agricultural cycle. Because people could not explain feats of nature, they developed rituals around these events that were akin to calling out spells with descriptive movement. During pagan times, fire was thought to be cleansing, so boys would jump over bonfires to shed evil spirits. Left over from that time are male dancers who now perform jumping tricks and athletic leaps.

After Christianity arrived in 988-989 AD, belief in mysticism weakened, as it was discouraged and sometimes banned. Ukrainians adapted to this new belief system and fit their dances into it by focusing on social dancing and thematic subjects like everyday occurrences.

In order to portray life as it was, Ukrainian dancers started using props like aprons, hats, swords and lances to express their situations in a kind of pantomime. There was no poetry or text used, so a wide range of storytelling expressions were developed solely through movement.

Village life in the dances emulated real life, so behaviour in each movement was especially important, and still is. Females maintained their modesty by clapping their hands and keeping their emotions in check, for example, instead of doing high kicks or jumps; males displayed their agility with fantastic athletic feats and creative new ways to express their pride.

Polite mannerisms of the day were articulated during each dance: a boy would never take a girl by the waist until after she had signalled that he could do so and he showed his pride of her beauty and poise by being attentive and respectful. Although today's roles for men and women have changed, these traditions are still a signature part of Ukrainian dancing.

This transformation in how people danced was developing during the formation of Ukrainian nationality, giving their dancing a solid foundation of identity going forward. The steps that were created at this time formed the basic structure that future choreographers would eventually follow.

There were a few external influences as many other parts of the world were seeing an upswing of social dancing. The quadrille, polka and waltz were influencers and choreographers would even stage quadrilles in certain villages. But these outside styles never took a real hold. Villagers were more likely to try them out and add their own folksy twist to them than to outright adopt them.

Ukrainian national theatre was also adapting, with shows becoming more progressive and mirroring life in Ukraine; folk dancing was turning into stage dancing, with a non-participatory audience. Dance ensembles all over the country took advantage of this change and popped up by presenting melodramas that combined acrobatic elements and Russian, Polish and gypsy influences.

Vasyl Mykolayovych Verkhovynets (Kostiv) was the first to write a book about Ukrainian dance as an art form, called "Theory of the Ukrainian Folk Dance" in 1919. He developed a way to transcribe dance onto paper, which helped to record village dances, and also made it possible for people all over the country (and world) to learn them and put them up on stage as performances. This led to the creation of many more dance troupes, lessons being formally taught in studios and innovators like Pavlo Virsky, who created whole concert programs. Pavlo's career is remembered by the re-naming of the state dance ensemble of Ukraine to the "National Honoured Academic Dance Ensemble of Ukraine named after P. Virsky."

When Ukrainians first began immigrating to Canada in the late 1800s, an estimated 170,000 arrived between 1892 and 1914. Most settled in western Canada in the aspen parkland that stretches from central Alberta to south central Manitoba. The vegetation here resembles that in the sub-Carpathian foothills and Carpathian Highlands of Halychyna and Bukovyna, where many of the immigrants came from.

The man heralded for bringing Ukrainian dance to Canada and making it "a big deal," Tammy tells me, is a man named Vasyl Avramenko, mentioned earlier by Serhij. He travelled through parts of Europe before receiving permission to enter Canada in 1925, when he taught groups of students Ukrainian dance from the motherland. Step by step he would go over a dance until the group could do it on its own. He would then appoint a new leader who was charged with the group before moving onto the next town and starting all over again.

As word spread, his groups started performing and, eventually, teaching others the same steps. This foundation that could be passed on from teacher to student enabled the art of Ukrainian dance to spread all over the world. He went on to make the first Ukrainian language film to be produced in the United States, *Natalka Poltavka*, and performed at the

White House. Vasyl is often called the "Father of Ukrainian Dance" for his dedication to spreading the art outside of Ukraine.

Transplanting traditional dances to a new country, though, inevitably alters them. As Serhij talked about girls doing the boys' roles, Tammy agrees that there have been changes, but in Vohon, they haven't experimented with gender roles.

"We're very traditional in the roles [of male and female]. Sometimes we say that the women have the background tree look, not to be putting anybody down, I mean, women have phenomenal solos, but the guys do the flips and the cartwheels. Spin, spin, spin, as a female, I can appreciate that, but when someone does 20 splits in the air…! So I've seen some groups have the females do the guys part.

"Tonight, during the *kolomyika*, you might see some girls doing the guys stuff, because it's a free thing, it's not stylized like on the stage, so they have that flexibility and that freedom to do whatever they want. Because folk is just for the people, right, for themselves and for their entertainment, and that's where the *kolomyika* fits so well in a folk dance theme.

"Stylized I would agree with [Serhij] in terms of dance on the stage in Canada because we do push the envelope more so than they would in Ukraine. It is very prescriptive. Whereas [here], 'let's try it, let's see where it goes.' And so I think because of the other dance styles in Canada, it does give us the freedom.

"However, I did see something on YouTube from Ukraine that was very modern-esque, but they were wearing Ukrainian dance costumes. So maybe Ukraine is also now moving into a new realm. Because of technology and because they can see things on YouTube and various other digital pieces, why can't we explore it? Now, the borders are coming down all across the world. We can see dance from all over. I think that's what's happening there, too."

But there are times when groups go too far. "I know one group that [tried something new] and they changed choreography after they premiered the number because they went way too far modern and I had a *baba* sitting in front of me and she was like, 'Agh.' I remember hearing her say, 'That's not Ukrainian dance.' For her. Because we're still part of that tradition, so it's interesting. Because some people want you to push it but yet, do you push it?"

Tammy's mention of the *kolomyika* was exciting, as I knew that the culmination of the whole weekend here in Jasper was the *kolomyika* (also spelled *kolomyjka* or *kolomeyka*) on Saturday night. This is when everyone will join in a circle and show off their best moves.

Back at the dinner table, we have finished our meals, the wine has slowed and the bishop and the sisters have said their farewells for the evening. Silly wedding-type tunes are being played by the band – think pop hits, easy listening and even the Macarena – as I wait patiently for my turn to be Ukrainian for a few songs in the *kolomyika*.

Just before the clock hits midnight, there is a distinct change in the air: the music revs up about 10 Ukrainian notches, the atmosphere is jolted with a new buzz of energy and everybody knows exactly what is happening. I hear, "*kolomyika!*" and half of the room jumps up out of their seats. Anastasia nods, "yes, this is it" and off we go to the centre of the room to join the circle. Kids are scrambling to find their way to the person they want to stand beside; teenagers and adults are gathering hands together and the oldest in the crowd stay seated to cheer from the sidelines.

At first, we all hold hands and move around in a circle, setting the tone for what is to come. Eventually everyone stops in place and begins clapping to the music. The first teenaged boy bravely bounds into the centre and does a few Russian split jumps that incite the first round of cheering. Next up is a little boy who skims the inside of the circle on his hands and feet, like a scuttling crab, kicking his legs out in front of him in time with the music. The first girl then takes centre stage and shows off her spins and turns, whipping around as fast as the rhythm can carry her and finishing without a single dizzy waver.

The rest of us in the circle are still clapping like mad, some calling out to the dancers and encouraging their friends to give it a try. A lot of the dancers I had seen perform earlier in the evening are completely at home in the centre, showing off the tricks and steps they have worked on all year, but there are many in the circle who also make their mark by pulling out a retro dance move, like the running man, to much hooting and hollering. The *kolomyika* is probably the closest form of Ukrainian traditional folk dance today. Although the moves are often not "folk," the concept certainly is.

This is just the warm up, though. Four guys in their late teens step into the circle with smiles on their faces. They clasp forearms in a small circle formation and begin walking in a clockwise direction. Circling around and alternating two at a time, they press down on the others' hands, leaning forward and flinging their legs back in a backwards windmill. They repeat it over and over again in a swirl of flinging legs. It looks like there is no support for the guys flinging their legs out behind them, a sure way to fall flat on their faces, but they support each other with the strength of their forearms. Their effort is rewarded with slaps on their backs from their friends.

All the while the band is still bellowing out music. They don't stop playing for the entire *kolomyika*, keeping a running melody pumping through the room and adding their own flourishes and accents as they feel necessary.

By this time, there is a scattering of high heels around the circle, their owners able to participate more fully without their constraints. It is mostly teenagers leaping into the centre, obviously having practised their steps and created group tricks before arriving. This next generation of Ukrainian-Canadians are happy to continue their traditions and challenge each other to come up with new ways to express their identity. Could this happen without using dance as the medium?

What will become the grand finale is a Ukrainian wedding staple. As Tammy had told me earlier, "In weddings, we throw the groom in a *kolomyika*. The groom is thrown from one side to the other by guys. That's just what we do," she had shrugged with a smile.

A group of young men converge in the centre of the circle and create two lines facing each other, with one off to the side representing the groom. After they all clasp hands with the person opposite to them, the "groom" is picked up on one end and flung high up in the air to the other end. Back and forth they fling him like they are popping crowd surfing popcorn, the musicians adding dramatic clangs on the cymbals every time the "groom" flies through the air. They are spurred on by the boisterous circle begging for more, as well as the crowd still sitting at their tables.

I ask Tammy why Ukrainians *need* to dance, why dance is one of the biggest parts of her culture, something that holds together the history of a people who struggled with warring neighbours, immigrated in droves to the Canadian prairies and were determined to keep the memories of their homeland alive.

"I think the topic you're exploring, dance, to me it's a lifeline. I mean, that's probably why I danced for 30 years and I'm still teaching dance, right? If we do not have dance in the Ukrainian community, I don't know. I don't know. It would be like this huge void. It'd be huge. It's too embedded in who we are."

I see it in the smiles of the children, proudly wearing their folk costumes and getting ready to go on stage; I see it in the eyes of their parents, eager for their children to know their own culture; and I see it in the contemplative looks of the grandparents, content that their pioneering work will not be lost or forgotten in this vast country.

8 British Columbia: Visitors Who Never Left

I dash into the Museum of Anthropology in Vancouver just as the performance is about to begin, brushing off wisps of snow from my clothing that have dusted the early spring evening. Scanning the Great Hall, there are portable black chairs set up in a "C" shape, the empty space in the centre a spill over from the carpeted area that will act as a stage to my right. Heads turn casually my way as I search for an empty seat, failing to find one in the audience.

Straight ahead of me, three spots in, I finally see one vacant chair in the first row. It's not being saved with someone's jacket or scarf, so I scurry across the stage and make a gesture to the gentleman sitting next to it to see if it is indeed free. He looks momentarily startled but motions for me to sit down. I dart into the chair and clumsily take off my jacket just as the show begins.

Elder Larry Grant of the traditional Musqueam First Nation comes out to say a few welcoming words as I settle into my seat. He thanks the other elders who are present, who are sitting to my right, and who are subsequently honoured in each of the opening speeches. I look over at them as I clap with the audience and notice that they are dressed in full family regalia and sit on a handmade wooden bench with clan insignia.

Seeing those who directly surround me for the first time, I realize that I have mistakenly sat in the middle of the section reserved for the family who has founded this festival and are regarded as an integral part of reviving First Nations culture in northwestern British Columbia. Thinking I should move, I am about to get up and find a place to stand at the back of the room when I notice the warm smiles from those around me have nothing behind them but a welcoming spirit. I sit back down, grateful for their graciousness at having me join them.

I am at the second annual *We Yah Hani Nah Coastal First Nations Dance Festival* in Vancouver and tonight is the opening gala and premier of the *Visitors Who Never Left*, a site-specific piece by the Dancers of Damelahamid that tells the history of their origins. This family dance group, of the Royal Dakhumhast House of the Gitxsan Nation, performs pieces that illustrate the creation story specific to their ancestors.

This work is based on the book of the same name by Chief Kenneth B. Harris and his mother, Mrs. Irene Harris, which captures in print the oral myths and stories of the people of Damelahamid. Near present day Hazelton and the Skeena River in northern B.C., this is where, according to Gitxsan history, Damelahamid was born.

In the book, the myths go that a young woman was taken by her husband-to-be to "a beautiful and a strange place" not on earth. They arrived at his father, the chief's, house where the woman was bathed and the water peeled away her skin and made her appear different, made everyone there appear different. Her husband-to-be accepted her as his wife and, although she was a virgin, she gave birth to two boys and a girl. The boys were given the names Liggeyoan, Akagee and the girl was named

Goestella and given the powers of miraculous healing.

Their grandfather gave them instructions to go to earth to avenge their people, who had been killed by the people of the village across the river, starting with killing the chief. Once this was done, the grandfather would place the children in a new and beautiful land called Damelahamid. There, the children would have to build a new home to very precise specifications and place in front of it a small pole that their grandfather had given them to take. The pole would grow all by itself and would become known as *gilhast*, the first totem pole. The children were given a *hawlhz-ganku*, a decorated box, filled with the small pole, a *lan num ghide*, which is an ermine-fur hat with "brilliant stones," and a *tja-hō*, a baton for use in their revenge.

So the two boys and the girl were placed on earth where their ancestor's village used to be. The boys canoed to the other village and killed the chief with the *tja-hōi* and made war until all that was left of the village was poplar twigs. The three siblings then explored the rest of the river, destroying anyone they came into contact with.

After some time camping out along the river, word came during the middle of the night that they must go to their chosen place, to Damelahamid, and they were transported there, leaving behind the *tja-hō* because there was so much killing and "it was meant for them to forget it." They built their home to the specifications their grandfather had given them, planting the pole in front of it. The next morning the pole had grown until it pierced the sky and was the beginning of a new clan, the Gisgahast.

The present day Dancers of Damelahamid are led by Margaret Grenier, the Artistic Director, who has spearheaded this festival from a deep passion to see her family's history kept alive. *The We Yah Hani Nah* festival began in 1967 by her parents as the *Haw yah hawni naw* festival in Prince Rupert. "When the culture was starting to come out of hiding again," Margaret begins, "the mayor realized the importance of First Nations history to his city and the surrounding area, and he invited Ken and Margaret Harris to start an event to share their traditions. The two agreed and created what was to become an annual festival for the next 19 years."

"Having followed the awakening of our traditions after the lifting of the Potlatch Ban," the current festival website states, "the purpose of the festival was to build community amongst the many people working to regain their ancestral dance and art traditions and a source of inspiration for the young artists."

When the family decided to move to Vancouver, the festival was put into the hands of the couple's youngest daughter, Margaret Grenier, and her generation of Gitxsan people. This piece, the *Visitors Who Never Left*, honours the work that Chief Kenneth B. Harris, Margaret's grandmother, and her grandmother's brother, put into the book.

The significant title of both the book and the performance piece signifies several things: there are a few visitors who are said to have come to Damelahamid. The first visitor who never left is an ancestor who is said to have come with the aboriginal people from heaven and is destined to be with them until the end of time to remind them of where they came from. Another visitor that comes from one of their oral histories is a temporary visitor that is said to have been welcomed into the house and was given a place of honour at the centre of the home. The third visitors are all the children of Damelahamid, the people who are associated with this lineage and are all visitors who never left.

The group chose several special songs to tell their story, all of which the family grew up singing. "They're what has been passed down, they're what we've inherited." Margaret leans in, "It's not really us choosing them, but it's what we've inherited that defines what it is we present and how we tell our history. The ones that were chosen for *Visitors Who Never Left* were chosen because those were the key songs that were done for us as children, that we grew up with, that were really signature to our family."

The piece was specifically choreographed to be performed in the Great Hall at the Museum of Anthropology with adaptations of the dances to respond to the space. The most pressing reason for the creation of the work was the realization that the younger generation had finite time left with their parents. This work is to honour their parents' and grandparents' contributions to the family's life and to share those gifts with the public. I would learn later that Margaret's father passed away in March of 2010 and this performance was the last one he would share with the family.

As the evening progresses, the dancers tell the story of K'i'y hasgaltxw, the one-horned mountain goat of Stekyawden; Neeth pun nim guljeb, a welcoming to the land of Damelahamid; Waydetai, who saved the people from the great flood; Medeekum juyax, the huge monster sea bear; Hiswildoget, the female warrior *nochnoch* (spirits capable of taking on different human or animal forms); Limk simhalyte, the Chief's headdress song that calls upon the Heavenly Father to bear witness to this event; and Benii exit, a Hagwilget prophet who foretold the coming of the Europeans.

The performance is mesmerizing. Singers sing from the depths of their bellies and drummers beat their drums to keep the dancers in rhythm. The family-made regalia glows with handmade pride and attention to the smallest detail; the children's smiles and giggles creep onto the faces of every member in the audience. I clap and tap my foot along with the drums as the family members beside me sing the songs they know so well. As much as this piece is telling the story of the people of Damelahamid, it is also a celebration of a culture that was nearly lost.

The Gitxsan, like other First Nations, performed songs and dances in their feast halls as an integral part of defining their art and culture. The dance group's literature states that, "All Gitksan belong to one of four clans or phratries: the Gisgahast, Ganada, Lukiboo and Lasxeek. The first clan, the Gisgahast, 'the people of the pole' was named in reference to the creation story. More clans developed to regulate spouse selection and prevent incest.

"The second clan was the Ganada, the frog clan. The people of the Ganada established themselves across the Skeena river from the Gisgahast where the village of Kitan`max is now located. The third clan is the Lukiboo, the wolf clan, which was established where the city of

Prince Rupert is presently located. The forth clan is the Lasxeek, the eagle clan, which originated on Haida Gwaii. The people of a clan share common ancestors, crests, and privileges."

Margaret's grandmother, Irene Harris, was the last in her family to have experienced a truly traditional upbringing within the feast system. Her knowledge of the Potlatch Ban and subsequent cultural revival in the 60s was passed down to her son, Chief Kenneth B. Harris, and now onto Margaret's generation, who continues the festival her parents began in 1967.

The group still makes their own regalia: "Everything is made from within the family," Margaret maintains. "In my grandmother's generation when the Potlatch Ban was lifted, she had a few items that were hidden within her walls that were saved, but besides those few items, there wasn't anything. Even when you listen to the old songs, you hear that they're even drumming by hitting their laps or pots. But we have, over time, worked very hard from one generation to the next, and there's only been two generations since then, to really grow and develop what we have."

The Dancers of Damelahamid's dances have not just been created in the last few years, but go back generations untold. The songs, dances and regalia all represent the authority of the Chief that they belong to. They are created to tell the story that belongs to that Chief, in this case Chief Kenneth B. Harris, *Hagbegwatku* (which translates to "first born of the nation"), and the story in itself reveals many things: it states who they are, it identifies them as part of a house and family unit, and it gives an exact location of where that story takes place. The dances were created to be passed down from generation to generation, but they are kept alive today by performing them to public audiences.

"I think, in Canada, there are a lot of stereotypes still that need to be overcome and I believe that the only way to bridge those distances is to be able to experience who you are, through art, in a way that is tangible for other people, something they can experience and come to know," Margaret explains. "Not just from knowledge but from, you know, it'll touch their hearts, it'll touch their minds, it'll touch them in different ways, and I think that's a very important part of how these songs are presented. I guess you could say there is some development that has happened, because it's not static, but it's also not redeveloped, it's something that's still part of our community."

We Yah Hani Nah continues throughout the weekend and showcases groups from as far north as Alaska and the Yukon. Working with other nations has been extremely rewarding for Margaret. "I think it's something that builds really great strength. There's support for one another and it revitalizes you and makes you feel not so isolated on your own. We all have such strong mandates to do what we do and it's very difficult work because there's not just the art itself but you're overcoming so much social and political struggle to do what you do. Then making choices and there's protocol, there's so much that just drains you, so when you have the support of your peers, I think it's a wonderful way to refresh and inspire one another…

"It's been a very powerful experience for us because it means so much to us. We've had a wonderful response and welcome from the local First Nations, which is of great importance to us. We've also had a wonderful response from the artists. So that has made our ability to do it even possible. This is only the second year, so it's been a lot of work to get the momentum put behind the festival and the recognition that we need to bring people to come and see it. But we've had wonderful audiences both years and we have really great dance groups dancing with us, so it's been incredibly powerful and fulfilling work and beyond even what you think might happen year to year."

For the groups that are performing this weekend, their dancing is creating a rope, made stronger by supporting each other and by being supported publicly. When a community develops a sturdy rope to hold onto, it can then begin to build a powerful network that can weave into today's tapestry of societies, making us all that much richer.

Beginning from the youngest, Gitxsan children don't learn how to dance; they grow up *immersed* in it. Most of them would never remember learning, they would just remember knowing. In that knowledge lies the documentation of a people who have fought their way back from invasion, residential schools, a disconnection from their language and customs, and are now beginning to let go of their shame and share the culture that was taken from them. With dance, all of the emotions that have been kept inside for many years can be unleashed to a whole new audience of witnesses.

I think Margaret said it best when she told me that the most important reason for the work that she does is to maintain and respect her family's identity and heritage. Even if people can't understand their language, culture or protocol, there can still exist a respect that allows us to listen in the right way.

"It is a very challenging space to be in. It's something that brings you great joy but also brings a great struggle. It can be very discouraging sometimes, but I think what keeps us going is the mandate to see something corrected. I believe there was a strong shift that happened for our people and we have tried very hard to hold onto what's important to us throughout, what I would still call a colonial period. I don't think we've past that yet."

"We [dance] to see something carry forward that we might have lost. And everyone who comes to *We Yah Hani Nah* and shares their songs and dances has something unique to offer and there is no other dance group, be it of the same nation or the same area, that can do what they do because they are representing their families and representing something unique. So everybody who sings and dances knows that if they don't, no one else will."

This reminds me of the countless untold stories that exist in Canada, some waiting for their chance to be shared, others protected from being revealed. I had been emailing back and forth with a few people in Haida Gwaii, the remote islands off the northwest coast of B.C. The Haida have lived here for possibly 13,000 years, flourishing from their close proximity to the sea. Flourishing, that is, until the same thing happened to this First Nation as it did countless other aboriginal groups across North America: during the 1880s and beyond, their culture was banned from being expressed and their beliefs were stifled in favour of learning Christian ways in residential schools, schools where many students were abused physically, emotionally and sexually.

The Haida barely survived waves of population losses from diseases including small pox and tuberculosis brought over with the European traders. As John Valliant writes in his haunting book, *The Golden Spruce: A True Story of Myth, Madness and Greed*, the Haida population had dropped 95 per cent at one point from estimated pre-contact numbers.

When good-intentioned missionaries strode in to help the population by providing them with housing, clothes and food, they did so while pushing Christianity and smothering Haida beliefs. The Potlatch Ban in 1884 was the most extreme way to silence Haida culture. By not allowing them to demonstrate the rights and privileges of the host, or mark an important occasion with song and dance, the way they had been honouring life events since the beginning of their creation, they were spiritually defeated.

Half way up to Haida Gwaii from Vancouver is the tiny village of Alert Bay and the U'mista Cultural Centre, where an example of the effect of the ban can be clearly seen. *U'mista* means "the return of something important." The centre exists to find and repatriate the regalia that was taken from them during the Potlatch Ban era and to regain their Kwakwaka'wakw culture.

"We dance to celebrate life, to show we are grateful for all our treasures," the centre's website states. "We must dance to show our history, since our history is always passed on in songs and dances. It is very important to tell the stories in exactly the same way. We put our stories into songs and into dances so they will not change. They will be told the same way every time. We use theatre and impressive masks to tell our ancestor's adventures so the people witnessing the dance will remember it.

"The ceremony to tell our stories and to show social changes such as birth, marriage, name giving, standing up a new chief and death is called a Potlatch. In the Chinook language it means 'to give'. The people we invite are not only guests. They are also witnesses of our Potlatch and we give them presents for being a witness."

The centre's focus is on a particular potlatch that happened in 1921. It was hosted at nearby Village Island so those who attended could evade the Indian Agents who were enforcing the ban. Somehow, the agents still found them and 45 people were arrested and charged with crimes like dancing, having and receiving gifts, and giving speeches.

Agent Halliday, who made the arrests with a partner, confiscated regalia and other items from the potlatch and put them in a museum where he charged admission. Although illegal, he allowed that if tribes gave up all of their potlatch paraphernalia, those who were charged would receive only suspended sentences. Many "guilty" people reluctantly did so. Part of Halliday's new collection was then sold to a collector in New York, and other parts shipped to Victoria, Ottawa and Toronto.

Lillian Hunt, who now leads tours and training programs through U'mista, is proud of what they've accomplished by bringing much of that collection back, and knows the importance of the work she does.

"I was pretty young when [the Potlatch Ban and residential schools were] going on, so I wasn't all that connected, as it was my parent's and my grandparent's era that went through all these hard times, and the stigma and the trauma and all that. But now it's my generation that is moving this sort of project forward and my children's generation, who's now going into the legwork, and my grandchildren's generation who absolutely love it."

The older generation, "they want to be involved. It's very hard for them, absolutely, we've experienced that firsthand with our old people and what we refer to as elders-in-training, not quite in their 70s yet but still have big memories from the hardships that they suffered through throughout the era and what they remember.

"I was a little girl then, but I still remember my grandparents coming over to visit, not knowing back then that they had suffered through the residential schools system and lost their regalia – we have my grandfather's regalia in this cultural centre – only later on when we got older did we understand the impact on our family.

"But thanks to a lot of our people during that era, they continued to fight the fight and they stood their ground, got together and this is why we appreciate what we have today thanks to them.

"The lessons we get from the ancestors are embedded in thousands of years of history and this is what we still use today, what they have taught us, what is carried forward through all those generations because of the methods they developed during the developing of the ceremonies and all the laws. Everything that they built and provided for us is true testament to their strength and wisdom because this is what we still use today."

And this includes dancing. There is now a troupe, called the T'sasała Dance Group, who performs traditional Kwakwaka'wakw dances at the centre for visitors in July and August. Because many of the tribes are now extinct, they represent various tribes and languages by performing songs and dances in their traditional state. An important sacred dance is the *hamat'sa* (cannibal) dance, a re-enactment of a young man being possessed by a cannibal spirit and then returning to his human self.

As a child, Lillian remembers "the old ladies used to reach out and grab us as we were walking down the street. We were outside playing and they'd yard us into wherever they were sitting and teach us a thing or two! A handful of women just ran around, started gathering up the children and they arranged to get a space that was down in behind U'mista to start teaching the dancing and the language."

Those women are the reason these dances continue on. The resilience of the Kwakwaka'wakw people is the only way their traditions could have been kept alive and their culture not completely taken from them.

***

I reach Skidegate, one of two Haida villages in Haida Gwaii (formerly known as the Queen Charlotte Islands; the name was officially changed back to the modern Haida language in December 2009) just before the annual celebrations at the Haida Heritage Centre. This facility was officially opened in the summer of 2008 and is 4,924 square metres (53,000 square feet) with five timber longhouses, a museum, multipurpose rooms, a gift shop, a café, the Bill Reid Teaching Centre, the Carving Shed, the Canoe House and the Performing House.

Although I must leave before the celebrations, I am generously invited by Nika Collison and Natalie Fournier of the Hltaaxuulang Gud Ad K'aaju ("friends together singing") dance group, and Jason Alsop of the heritage centre, to witness the dance rehearsal for the event.

I walk into the centre on a Friday night. The sound of drum beats, the voices in song, children running and playing, and laughter spilling into the hallways leads me to the dancers. I turn the corner to see about 15 people gathered in the longhouse, each wearing different red and black regalia: black felt capes with a red border that has pearly white buttons edging it; black pants or skirts with a red panel or a raven design; some wear woven hats, others white and black bands around their heads; a few carry canoe paddles or hand drums and one young girl wears a red felt cape with moccasins and jeans.

I walk in and let them know who I am. Nika and Natalie welcome me warmly and gesture for me to enter the Performing House. Nika gathers the dancers and singers together and introduces me to the group. She asks me to share with them what I am doing here, so that everyone feels comfortable and can speak up if they have any objections.

I explain that I am here to witness their rehearsal so I can learn more about their traditional dances, and that I would like to take photos and video footage for my research. They ask me about where else I have been and what other types of dancing I am studying, and they all agree that I can photograph and video them.

They have been through this kind of introduction already in the last few days, as four young women are also setting up their cameras in the longhouse to capture the rehearsal. They have come to Haida Gwaii on an expedition made possible through the National Geographic Young Explorers program and funded by the Ritt Kellogg Memorial Fund out of Colorado College to explore cultural preservation and conservations issues, and environmental activism.

The young explorers spent their first 17 days here sea kayaking along the east coast of Gwaii Haanas National Park (*gwaii haanas* meaning "Islands of Beauty" in Haida), the southernmost part of Moresby Island, and this month have been hanging around the Village of Queen Charlotte interviewing those who have fought to protect the islands and activists who are still working for its betterment.

The Performing House is a gorgeous cedar longhouse-like space, with three steps on all sides descending into a "pit." The Haida people are divided into the Raven and Eagle clans, and a large cloth design depicting those animals is hanging at the front of the room. Bright sunlight blasts through the open doorways on either side of it and the high ceiling expands the room to feel larger than it is.

Without further ado, the chatter settles down and the group readies to practice their first dance. This is the Chief's Peace Dance, using Chief Cumshewa's song. Cumshewa was a Haida village that once stood on the northern shore of Cumshewa Inlet on Moresby Island. A dozen drummers and singers stand along one side of the longhouse steps in a sea of black and red regalia, their beige hand drums and wooden paddles moving in contrast.

The "Chief" enters the pit area to the steady pounding of the drums. He wears a yellow, blue and black cape with white fringes hanging from the bottom, and a red headdress with a yellow mask on the front and eagle feathers dangling down the sides and back of his head; on his legs are matching leggings around his calves with more white fringes.

His bare feet are spread out wide on the wooden floor and his knees are bent in a half seated position, half bouncing and half jumping slightly off the ground to each beat. In his right hand he holds a branch and every time the drummers make an emphasis with a long beat and the singers' voices lower in an abrupt tone, the "Chief" dips his head in the direction of his right arm, which also dips like he is tapping someone with a wand. This is a way for the Chief to welcome guests to the event and he spreads eagle feathers as a sign of peace.

Although a Chief's Dance is performed on many occasions, the Hltaaxuulang Gud Ad K'aaju dance group doesn't have a set repertoire of dances, like a regular troupe would, because each dance is ceremonial rather than for show. "It really depends on the ceremony we're performing," Nika tells me, "because we create ceremonies specific to the event at hand. Sometimes it might be a general performance, where we're honouring the Eagle side of the nation and the Eagle spirit, or it could be about the origin of the Eagle, so it depends on what dance we're doing."

Although each ceremony is different, Nika explains that the bases of the dances themselves are ones that they learned early on. "The principle behind the dancing and the singing has been passed down, predominantly unbroken – I mean, there's been lots of different things that we've faced over the decades, that have tried to stop our ceremonies – but for the most part they've been handed down. Of course, because we are a live and evolving culture, that means we do develop new dances as well. But they're always based, or speak in those original traditions, so that when we do move forward in a modern context, it's not just all willy nilly."

And that goes for the songs, too, which are also passed down and learned from parents and grandparents. "In particular, right now, it's so important that we can bring the old songs back out because of that time – I call it the silent years, from population loss right through to the 1950s when they finally lifted the Potlatch Ban, that was a long era, 1884 through 1950 where any visual or external practicing of our culture was outlawed in one form or another – so to be able to sing our old songs and bring them back out into youth is really important.

"That being said, we don't know all of our traditional songs' original functions anymore, so we have to re-study them and work with the elders to decide how best to apply them in a contemporary fashion. There are new songs being composed, again because we're a living culture. We can't just sing about things that happened in the far past.

"When we do a dance, it's a ceremony and it's to mark the occasion that is taking place. If it's in a potlatch, it's to demonstrate the rights and privileges that the host has, or to mark that occasion through some form of song and dance. So that's what song and dance is, it's ceremony. But just because it's ceremony doesn't mean it can't be fun or funny. I think a lot of people think, when they hear 'ceremony,' they're like 'Oh, we must be quiet and hang our heads and be super serious for 10 hours' and, yes, there are ceremonies like that, but there are also other ceremonies… Many years ago we moved away from the standard, 'We'll do the Eagle and the Raven and the Chief.' We have to put meaning back into it and tell stories with it, and that's what we're doing now."

The next dance I see is the story of the Bear Mother, with a man dressed in a full bearskin, complete with the head. The story goes that a young woman is out picking berries and becomes angry at the bears for eating all of them. In her irritation, she ends up slipping in bear feces and gets even madder, cursing the bear. So she calls for her husband and he comes to carry her home. It turns out that he's really a bear transformed to look like her husband and he takes her back to his bear village. In the end she winds up having two children who are half human and half bear, "which is why we know we are related to the black bears and are adamantly against commercial sport hunting of bears," Nika says.

Stories like this incorporate the group members' own suggestions, as well as tradition, to tell them. "Our particular dance group is very… I lead it and I teach it, but that doesn't mean I know everything," Nika laughs. "We often bring in elders or other knowledge holders and then, of course, people in our troupe themselves are knowledge holders and they have ideas to help build whatever ceremony we're working on.

"It doesn't mean that every suggestion thrown forward is accepted, though. The last ceremony we did was the end of winter, just about two weeks ago, and it was a 16 year old boy who got the idea for the basis of our ceremony. So people can put forward ideas. I can't speak for all

Haidas, but our group is not so much a caste system, do you know what I mean? There's not some all-knowing leader. Everyone brings different levels of knowledge. We all have grandparents at home, or aunties and uncles that have taught us things, so we might be in [rehearsal] and I'm choreographing something and maybe someone will say, 'Hey, my [nana] told me this, try this with it'…

"Within our group, for example, I'm the group leader, and that's just because I've been doing it for over 12 years with this particular group. We kind of fall into the roles. There are other people that are becoming really strong song leaders or really strong soloists; what I try to do as the leader of the group is I try and watch where the strengths are naturally coming out and then encourage them in that area.

"So we have people that have naturally occurred as the mask caretakers, which is a pretty important role, or the speakers, the people that address the audience or the main mask dancers or lead singers. As the group leader, I watch these people and when I see them emerging I'm like, 'Hey, why don't you try this?' and then they grow more. It's because historically this kind of stuff would have been done within a clan, which we still have, but there's so much of our societal ways that have been changed through modernization and assimilation and cultural genocide and everything else, that we have other ways of watching.

"Long ago, elders from the clan would watch the youth and see where they're starting to have their strengths come out, so now I've just sort of evolved as a clan singer within my clan because it's been my passion and it's something that I've taken seriously for years and studied and worked with elders, but maybe 100 years ago they would have watched me and identified that in me early on and raised me as a young girl with that. Do you know what I mean? So now what I'm doing in the group is I watch the group and I'm like, 'That person is an amazing soloist, they just need a little bit more support' or 'This person is becoming an excellent speaker and they need to be the one addressing the crowd.' And people are really just coming out of it in that way."

The last dance the group practises features individuals who have grown into certain roles, each representing a different animal or supernatural being that the Haida revere as inextricable parts of their daily lives. The first one out is a man dressed in the bearskin I saw earlier, hulking across the room. Following him is a butterfly, then a dogfish with a turquoise mask and a long blanket as a cape.

A very tiny beaver then emerges, with a large mask covering his face, and a slightly larger wolf comes out wearing a wolf skin. The Foam Woman, SGuulu Jaad, who the Raven clans originate from, has an elaborate mask with long white hair and a flowing green cape. Lastly comes the delicate hummingbird with a turquoise blanket as a cape and a carved wooden beak, and the charismatic frog that leaps up and down from a crouching position.

"The dancers themselves, like the mask dancers, they're not simply putting on a mask and acting like whatever they're embodying," Nika explains. "They have to really try and put themselves into that place of being. Either let the mask take them over or them coming into the mask. It's really important to be able to hear what they have to say about the choreography of the piece. And also so that they can react within the moment, if they need to… If they're dancing an Eagle, they're instructed to watch Eagles and study Eagles, not just that they fly, but everything about it. And it doesn't mean that all dancers do that, but that's what we encourage. The best mask dancers, you can tell when they're really working on their position, their responsibility."

It is also important that the clans make their own regalia, to keep them connected to the songs and dances, which are given out on important dates. "Predominantly, I'd say an overriding thing in our nation," Nika continues, "is that the original milestones of a child's life, say puberty and different things like that, and the ceremonies that mark them have been replaced, not purposely, but just over time, by graduations. Nowadays, at least in Skidegate, children, when they graduate nursery school, they get a blanket, like a dance blanket, and then when you graduate grade seven you get a vest or a blanket, and then when you graduate grade 12 you get another blanket, and when you graduate university you get another blanket.

"So the milestones of a person's growth in life have morphed into graduation dates as opposed to different stages in a person's life. Although, we're trying to bring back the old ways, but not to replace the new ways, because the new ways are good, too, and applicable to this day and age. So people acquire them that way or sometimes, like, I've made regalia for some of my closest clan sisters because I just love them and I want them to have good regalia. It really depends. Some people will make their own regalia but usually you're given it, but it's become more and more common now for people to make it. If they need a vest, they'll make themselves a vest."

Going forward, there are still many changes that the Haida will have to fight for and adapt to, as they have been doing since contact. One of the challenges now is to make sure that songs and dances are remembered and kept alive.

As Nika points out, "We actively work with our elders in Skidegate to ensure that our ancient songs are translated properly and transcribed into an alphabet that we can read, because we didn't have an alphabet years ago, right? And so that we can properly learn new songs and their meanings and their original intents where those still exist: who owns them? When to properly use them? How to properly use them? There are so many rules around songs and dances. Most are either individually or clan owned and if they're not, then they're collectively owned by the nation."

Although land claims debates most often make the headlines when it comes to First Nations news, these culturally significant components are equally as important to the future of all the nations. As history has proven, without culture, people have to reach out for self-destructive coping devices, struggling to make sense of fitting into someone else's beliefs. Now that we know better (right?), why would we force anyone to fit into a mould they don't fit into?

The most common thought I had when interviewing all of the aboriginal people I did for this book was that it's utterly impossible for them to get back what they have lost. Their identities were almost erased for so many years, so it's hopeless to think they will be able to salvage their culture. How can that culture still be alive?

And yet, despite a multi-decade assault on who they are, the Haida, the Gitxsan, the Kwakwa̲ka'wakw, all aboriginal people, have been fighting for their lives, often underground where no one could silence them. These incredible people have endured what should have killed their spirits and instead, they adapted, did what they needed to do to survive, and now work to remember what they were told they had to forget.

Everyone I spoke with was living their culture, seeing to it that it didn't die. It lives in them, in their children, their grandchildren and, hopefully, in all who come after them. It lives everyday.

I am biased because I grew up and still live in British Columbia, but it is one of the most dazzling places on this planet. It's easy to be mesmerized by the mysterious mountaintops, the dramatic waterways and the wildlife that runs untamed. Even with all this beauty, it is still the people and their stories that are the greatest asset we have here. They can only continue if they're able to reclaim their stories and dances, and from what I've learned from my research, they are doing just that.

Loved Dancing Through History?

Next up from author Lori Henry is a book about her experience growing up with *kapa haka*, which is Maori performing arts from New Zealand.

Photos

To see photos taken during Lori's travels across Canada,
visit Dancing Traveller Media's photo album at:
www.Flickr.com/photos/DancingTravellerMedia

Want to share your story?

Did she miss your favourite kind of dancing?
Do you have a dance story of your own from Canada?
Please share your dance and cultural experiences at:
www.LoriHenry.ca/DancingThroughHistory
or
www.Facebook.com/DancingTravellerMedia.

About the author

Lori Henry began Polynesian dancing when she was two years old. Although she also played ringette for many years, she ended up choosing to pursue dancing and trained in ballet, tap, jazz, modern, hip hop and contemporary styles. After high school, she attended Gastown Actors Studio in Vancouver to study theatre acting, and spent many years as a film actor.

After travelling solo to Paris in 2002, Lori caught the travel bug and began building on her growing number of writing assignments to embark on a career as a travel writer. Her work has been published in *Readers Digest Canada*, WestJet's *up! magazine*, *Western Living*, *British Columbia magazine*, *FLARE*, *VIA destinations*, *West*, *VIA magazine* (an AAA publication), *Spa*, *USAToday.com*, *Gateways* (Carnvial Cruise Lines), among many others. She has also contributed to Fodor's *Nova Scotia & Atlantic Canada*, Explorer Publishing's *Vancouver Explorer* and Sasquatch Books' *Best Places Northwest guidebooks*.

Dancing Through History: In Search of the Stories that Define Canada is the first book in a series about indigenous dance and cultures around the world.

Find Lori Henry online:
Website: www.LoriHenry.ca
Twitter: @LoriHenry
Google+: www.gplus.to/LoriHenry
Facebook: www.facebook.com/LoriFHenry
LinkedIn: http://ca.linkedin.com/in/LoriFHenry

Find us online:

Website: www.DancingTravellerMedia.ca

Twitter: @DancingTravel

Facebook: www.Facebook.com/DancingTravellerMedia

Flickr: www.Flickr.com/photos/DancingTravellerMedia

Dancing Traveller
Publishing

Acknowledgements

As you can imagine, there are a country full of people who helped make this book possible. I will start with my family, who don't bat an eye anymore when I announce a new project. Especially my parents, who have always provided me with an intangible safety net, teaching me to take risks – creatively, financially and professionally – in everything that I do. I don't know how to live any other way now.

I want to thank all of the people I interviewed and whose words are found throughout this book. These are the people who are keeping the dances and stories alive. John Houston, Maria Illungiayok, Lois Suluk-Locke, Tukummeq Arnaq, Dettrick Hala, Jim Watson, Colin Watson, Joanne MacIntyre, Melanie from the Celtic Music Centre, Jane Rutherford, Barb Murrary, Jasmin and Alison Astle, Melena Rounis, Barb Nepinak, Joanne Soldier, Carl Stone, Yvonne Chartrand, Anastasia Martin-Stillwell, Serhij Koroliuk, Tammy Komarnisky Myskiw- Vohon, Margaret Grenier, Nika Collison and Lillian Hunt.

Crystal Pite, thank you for allowing me to re-print part of your International Dance Day message, which has spoken to me since the first time I read it in 2010, and Kristin Harris Walsh for allowing me to re-print some of your paper on Irish-Newfoundland step dancing.

To my editor, Lynn Robinson, who provided necessary feedback and helped catch the many errors that I overlooked. To my brother, Mike, for helping with some technical issues. You know what I mean.

To my mom, Auntie Mona and Cori Caulfied: you read the manuscript before anyone else and provided me with advice that shaped the book. Robin Esrock: thank you for agreeing to read the manuscript and for your kind and encouraging words. James & Francesca Szuszkiewicz: thanks for your important contributions to the cover design.

A big thank you to the Canadian Tourism Commission (Elyse Mailhot), who sponsored a lot of my airfare to research this book, and the tourism boards and organizations that hosted me on my travels. They are: Tourism Nunavut, the Alianait Arts Festival (Heather Daley), Tourism

Nova Scotia (Pam Wamback and Randy Brooks), Feis An Eilein, Gaelic College, Highland Village Museum (Jim Watson and Rodney Chaisson), Celtic Music Centre, Paul Gallant of La Swing du Suete, Tourism New Brunswick (Heather MacDonald-Bossé), Fredericton Tourism (Stacey Russell), New Brunswick Highland Games (Melanie Laird), Tourism Quebec (Magalie Boutin), Tourism Montréal (Marie José Pinsonnault), La TOHU, National Circus School (Marie-Pier Turgeon), Ontario Tourism Marketing Partnership (Helen Lovekin and Kattrin Sieber), The Great Spirit Circle Trail (Gladys King), Wikwemikong Cultural Festival, Travel Manitoba, Tourism Winnipeg (Janice Tober), Manito Ahbee (RoseAnna Schick), Tourism Saskatchewan (Carla Bechard), Tourism Saskatoon, John & Vicky of the John Arcand Fiddle Fest, Vesna Festival (Klarissa Koamrnicki), Travel Alberta, Tourism Jasper, Fairmont Jasper Park Lodge (Lori Cote), Ukrainian Cultural Heritage Village, Aboriginal Tourism Association of British Columbia, Haida Heritage Centre (Jason Alsop), We ya hani nah Coastal First Nations Dance Festival (Margaret Grenier), and Museum of Anthropology (Jennifer Webb). Also to Cara Abrahams of Cirque du Soleil for giving me the go ahead to include Melena Rounis.

I will always be grateful to those who welcomed me to their city, town, village and hamlet, and who made travelling through Canada the pleasure that it is.

THANK YOU.

Travel Resources and Further Learning

Canada
- Canadian Tourism Commission: www.canada.travel
- Air Canada: www.aircanada.com
- WestJet: www.westjet.com
- *8th Fire* documentary (Aboriginal Canadians): www.cbc.ca/8thfire

Nunavut
- Tourism Nunavut: www.nunavuttourism.com
- First Air: www.firstair.ca
- Alianait Arts Festival: www.alianait.ca
- The Nunavut Handbook: www.arctictravel.com
- Adventure Canada: www.adventurecanada.com
- Artcirq: www.artcirq.org
- Isuma TV: www.isuma.tv
- Films by John Houston: *Songs in Stone, Nuliajuk, Diet of Souls, Kiviuq, The Most Interesting Group of People You'll Ever Meet, The White Archer.* www.houston-north-gallery.ns.ca/films
- NAIP (Nuummi Alikkusersuisartut Isiginnaartitsisartullu Peqatigiffiat): www.naip.dk (website in Greenlandic and Danish only)
- Tanya Tagaq: www.tanyatagaq.com

Newfoundland
- Newfoundland and Labrador Tourism: www.newfoundlandlabrador.com
- Vinland Music Camp and Sound Traditions: www.soundbone.ca
- DanceNL: www.dancenl.ca
- Intangible Cultural Heritage Coordinator: http://doodledaddle.blogspot.com
- Newfoundland & Labrador Folk Festival: www.nlfolk.com

Nova Scotia
- Tourism Nova Scotia: www.novascotia.com
- Destination Cape Breton Association: www.cbisland.com
- Highland Village Museum: www.museum.gov.ns.ca/hv
- Celtic Music Interpretive Centre: www.celticmusiccentre.com
- Féis an Eilein: www.feisaneilein.ca

- Gaelic College: www.gaeliccollege.edu
- Inverness County square dances: www.invernessco.com/dances.html
- Celtic Colours International Festival: www.celtic-colours.com

New Brunswick
- Tourism New Brunswick: www.tourismnewbrunswick.ca
- Fredericton Tourism: www.tourismfredericton.ca
- New Brunswick Highland Games: www.highlandgames.ca
- Scottish Official Board of Highland Dancing: www.sobhd.net

Quebec
- Tourism Quebec: www.bonjourquebec.com
- Tourism Montréal: www.tourisme-montreal.org
- Cirque du Soleil: www.cirquedusoleil.com
- La TOHU: www.tohu.ca/en
- National Circus School: www.nationalcircusschool.ca
- Les Colporteurs: www.lescolporteurs.com
- Montréal Complètement Cirque: www.montrealcompletementcirque.com
- Les Journées de la Culture: www.journeesdelaculture.qc.ca

Ontario
- Ontario Tourism Marketing Partnership: www.ontariotravel.net
- Manitoulin Tourism Association: www.manitoulintourism.com
- The Great Spirit Circle Trail: www.circletrail.com
- Wikwemikong Cultural Festival: www.wikwemikongheritage.org
- Wikwemikong unceded Indian reserve: www.wikwemikong.ca

Manitoba
- Travel Manitoba: www.travelmanitoba.com
- Tourism Winnipeg: www.tourismwinnipeg.com
- Manito Ahbee: www.manitoahbee.com
- Folklorama: www.folklorama.ca

Saskatchewan
- Tourism Saskatchewan: www.sasktourism.com
- Tourism Saskatoon: www.tourismsaskatoon.com
- John Arcand Fiddle Fest: www.johnarcandfiddlefest.com

- Vesna Festival: www.vesnafestival.com
- Pavlychenko Folklorique Ensemble: www.pfedance.com
- Back to Batoche Days: www.backtobatoche.org (in Métis chapter)

Alberta
- Travel Alberta: www.travelalberta.com
- Tourism Jasper: www.jasper.travel
- The Fairmont Jasper Park Lodge: www.fairmont.com/jasper
- Vohon Dance Ensemble: www.vohon.ca
- Ukrainian Cultural Heritage Village:
www.history.alberta.ca/ukrainianvillage

British Columbia
- Aboriginal Tourism Association of British Columbia:
www.aboriginalbc.com
- Tourism British Columbia: www.hellobc.com
- Tourism Vancouver: www.tourismvancouver.com
- Village of Alert Bay: www.alertbay.ca
- U'mista Cultural Society: www.umista.org
- Haida Gwaii Tourism Advisory Committee: www.gohaidagwaii.ca
- Haida Heritage Centre: www.haidaheritagecentre.com
- Dancers of Damelahamid / We ya hani nah Coastal First Nations
Dance Festival: www.damelahamid.ca
- Museum of Anthropology: www.moa.ubc.ca
- Compaigni V'ni Dansi: http://vnidansi.ca (in Métis chapter)
- Drive Dance Centre: www.drivedancecentre.com (in circus chapter)

Selected Bibliography

This collection of books, articles, films and websites provided me with much of the background information for this book. The rest I learned from firsthand interviews and is quoted throughout.

Aboriginal

- Boas, Franz. *The Central Eskimo*: University of Nebraska Press, 1964. (*The Central Eskimo* was originally published as part of the Sixth Annual Report of the Bureau of Ethnology, Smithsonian Institution, Washington, 1888.)
- Budak, Jasmine. "The Ringmaster." *Up Here magazine*, 2008. www.uphere.ca/node/305
-Coyes, Gregory, dir. *How the Fiddle Flows* (film): National Film Board of Canada, 2002.
- Evans, Michael Robert. *The Fast Runner: Filming the Legend of Atanarjuat*: University of Nebraska Press, Lincoln and London, 2010.
- Freeman, Lorraine, dir. *The Dances of the Métis (Li dawns di Michif)*: The Métis Resource Centre Inc. (now the Métis Culture & Heritage Resource Centre Inc.), 2001.
- Frideres, James S., and Gadacz, René R. *Aboriginal Peoples in Canada*: Pearson, 2007.
- George, Jane, et al. *The Nunavut Handbook: Travelling in Canada's Arctic*: Nortext, Iqluit, 2004.
- Gibbons, Roy W. *"La Grande Gigue Simple" and the "Red River Jig": A Comparative Study of Two Regional Styles of a Traditional Fiddle Tune*: Canadian Journal for Traditional Music, 1980.
- Harris, Kenneth B., and Robinson, Frances M.P. *Visitors Who Never Left: The Origin of the People of Damelahamid*: University of British Columbia Press, Vancouver, 1974.
- Hayes, Derek. Historical *Atlas of the Arctic*: Douglas & McIntyre Ltd., Vancouver, 2003.
- Laugrand, Frédéric, and Oosten, Jarich. "Quviasukvik: The celebration of an Inuit winter feast in the central Arctic." *Journal de la Société des Américanistes*, 2002: 203-225.
- Lussier, Antoine S., and Sealey, D. Bruce, eds. *The Other Natives: The Métis (Volume 2)*: Manitoba Métis Federation & Editions Bois-Brûlés, 1978.

- Magocsi, Paul Robert, ed. *Aboriginal Peoples of Canada: A Short Introduction*: University of Toronto Press, 2002.
- Payment, Diane P. *The Free People (Li Gens Libres): A History of the Métis Community of Batoche, Saskatchewan*: University of Calgary Press, 2009.
- Quick, Sarah. *The Social Poetics of the Red River Jig in Alberta and Beyond*: Dance in Canada, Vol. 30 No. 1, 2008.
- *Report of the Royal Commission on Aboriginal Peoples*: Royal Commission on Aboriginal Peoples, 1996.
- Sealey, D. Bruce, and Lussier, Antoine S. *The Métis Canada's Forgotten People*: Manitoba Métis Federation Press, 1975.
- Steckley, John L., and Cummins, Bryan D. Full Circle: *Canada's First Nations (second edition)*: Pearson, 2007.
- United States Department of the Interior. *Annual report of the Department of the Interior*: U.S. Govt. Printing Office, 1849, 1877.

Gaelic and Scottish
- *And They Danced* (film): Genuine Pictures, Ottawa, 2005.
- Flett, J.F., and Flett, T.M. *Traditional Dancing in Scotland* / Rhodes, F. *Dancing in Cape Breton Island Nova Scotia* (appendix): Routledge, 1964.
- Flett, J.F., and Flett, T.M. *Traditional Step-Dancing in Scotland* / Rhodes, F. *Step-Dancing in Cape Breton Island Nova Scotia*: Scottish Cultural Press, Edinburgh, 1996.
- Gibson, John G. *Traditional Gaelic Bagpiping: 1745-1945*: McGill-Queen's University Press, Montreal and Kingston, 1998.

Newfoundland and Irish
- Harris, Kristin M. *Integrating Vernacular Dance with Traditional Music: An Ethnographic Account of the Auntie Crae Band*: presented at SCDS 2003 conference; an earlier version was presented at Memorial University of Newfoundland in 2002.
- Walsh, Kristin Harris. *How Irish is Irish? Identity in Irish-Newfoundland Step Dancing*: Dance in Canada, 30-1, 2008.

Ukrainian
- Shatulsky, Myron. *The Ukrainian Folk Dance*: Kobzar Publishing Co. Ltd., Toronto, 1980.

- Staniec, Jillian. *Cossacks and Wallflowers: Ukrainian Stage Dance, Identity and Politics in Saskatchewan from the 1920s to the present*: a thesis submitted to the College of Graduate Studies and Research in partial fulfillment of the requirements for the degree of Master of Arts in the Department of History University of Saskatchewan, Saskatoon, 2007.
- Staniec, Jillian. *Remain True to the Culture?: Authenticity, Identity, and Association of United Ukrainian Canadians Sponsored Dance Seminars, 1971 to 1991*: Ethnologies, vol. 30 No 1, 59-76, 2008.

Index